Jenny's Surprise Ending

Ron Johnson

1st Edition

Contents

JENNY'S SURPRISE ENDING

Jenny's surprise ending is actually a continuation of Jenny's first book "Jenny's wheelchair". To understand what is going on in this book it would probably be best to read Jenny's wheelchair book first. I am sure you will enjoy both books because they are both a true story about My precious wife JENNY! I want to thank you for your interest in her life, as you will see we have a very special walk with Jesus and our love for Jesus continues to grow every day. Our love of Jesus is so strong; we believe Jesus gave His life for us to have life more abundantly, not just to be the atonement for sin. I pray that everyone that reads these books about Jenny will come to realize Jenny and I have the love of Jesus and that Jesus is a way of life, Jesus is the narrow path and the love of Jesus is a lot more than a bus ticket to heaven!!!!

November 1st, 2012

Jenny is amazing to me. Why? You might ask. In a word Jesus, yes Jesus, you see while talking to Jenny's doctor, this past summer; he said Jenny would not be here if not for the good care I am giving her. I know for a fact no one can add one moment to Jenny's life except God and I know Dr. Broderick was really saying; you're doing a great job. I love and respect Dr. Broderick. Jenny and I are privileged to know him. I think Dr. Broderick knows and I realize, helping Jenny live or keeping Jenny alive is beyond anything humanly possible. Dr. Broderick still sees Jenny once a year and prescribes her seizure medicine. I am so blessed that Jenny is only on one prescription and does not need or take any other medicine of any kind. I think Dr Broderick and I realize Jenny's life is in the hands of God. I know for sure I do! I give praise to you Jesus for Jenny's life! Jenny could not even smile if not for Jesus, I believe every breath we have is a gift from God. I believe Jenny is amazing because I believe even in this state she hears and is responding to the love of Jesus. I pray for more Jenny time!!!! I thank you Jesus for even more Jenny time!! I hear people say every day is a gift from God and I give praise to my Father God whom is the giver of life, through Jesus my brother.

In a way I feel sorry for doctors. You see they are limited to the knowledge they have about their specialty unless they have faith and trust in God for if they had their faith in God they too could move mountains. I know my faith and trust are in God. Like I said I respect doctors and I know they do great things for people every day. I'm actually happy they have no medicine for Picks disease. I don't think my faith in God would not be where it is today if the doctors had a cure.

I thank you Jesus for the desire to know you and seek you with all my heart. I thank You Jesus for the cure of Picks disease coming directly from you in the form of a healing! I thank you Jesus that I do not have why questions, you know like why is this happening, why is Jenny continually getting worse, etc. Instead I have hope in a miraculous healing, I have hope in the giver of life, and I know there is no such thing as death. So I know Jenny is going to live forever and she is healed right now! In fact I hear her stirring right now, thank You Jesus for life and for stirring awake my Jenny!

I believe Jenny and I are blessed to have this relationship with God. Anyone that has a relationship with God is truly blessed. I know as I grow up in my relationship with God and the more I study His life, the more freedom I see in Jenny's and my life. I believe most people think freedom is being able to do what you want to do. You know the world calls it (the pursuit of happiness). I've lived in campgrounds now almost four years. I see people trying to find happiness in traveling. Some are trying to escape their own children. Notice I said trying to find happiness. Traveling is just traveling. Seeing new and great places can bring happiness but like going to Kings Island it is momentary. I know the only way to true happiness is not seeking things that bring happiness but to seek God and He brings Joyfulness. I believe joyfulness is the opposite of happiness. Happiness comes from doing things for yourself and having others do things for you. Where Joyfulness comes from doing things for others. For example;

Jenny and I were camping next to a young couple. They had four children and seemed very happy. One night they knocked on our door and ask to come in. I said sure come on in and I ask what would you like to talk about. They looked a little surprised and then ask; how do you stay so happy? She said I see you taking care of you wife and she can do nothing for herself. You have literally put your life on hold to take care of her and you do it with such love. I simply told them I have Jesus in my life. My relationship with Jesus is my source of Joy! No one can take the Joy of knowing Jesus away.

They started telling me about their own childhoods. They both had a terrible past and truly terrible things had happened to them. I lessoned for about half an hour and ask if it made them

7

happy to talk about their past. They both said not really. I ask whom benefits form you talking about your past. They looked at me like you don't care do you? I said really I don't care about your past but I do care about your future. I said I like knowing your past history because it tells me you two are overcomers. Jesus loves when we overcome our past and Jesus loves when we fall in love with Him despite our past!

They went on to tell me how they have a lot of anger, which comes out at the worst times. Now they see some anger in their children and it is very disturbing to them. They talked about the curses being handed down from generation to generation. I interrupted them to ask, do you believe curses are handed down from generation to generation and if so are you powerless to stop it? If you are powerless to stop it then I guess the anger goes on and on. They looked at each other and then ask how do you stop it then?

I asked why Jesus came. To forgive us our sins they said. Yes and does He do that? Yes Jesus forgives and removes them as far as the east is from the west. If you really believe that Jesus forgives and removes are sins as far as the east is from the west why do you think they are still handed down from generation to generation? When you repent for a sin issue in your life, the sin is forgiven. Some people think the sin is forgiven but not forgotten. To them it can be handed down from generation to generation. Jesus said forgive them Father, they know not what they do. In your case you need to forgive your parents for they knew not what they were doing. Jesus came to be our example of how to live and how to forgive. I mean Jesus said Father forgive them when they were pounding the nails in his hands! So do you think you should forgive your parents for your terrible past?

Jesus showed us the importance of being born again. When we are born again we have new blood lines, that is we voluntarily switch bloodlines and have a new Father. Original sin is removed along with the curses of our earthly parents. So we are no longer tied to the past we are free to be who God created us to be!

I ask earlier who benefits form you dwelling on your past. They said I guess the devil. So whom do you want to please the devil or God? If you dwell on the past, it pleases the devil because you look at all the hurt and pain in your life over and over again, until the hurt seems too monumental to forgive! Jesus said what we fix our eye on we will become. Thinking about the past hurts you and benefits the devil, it pleases the devil, it makes it harder and harder to forgive and takes away your relationship with Jesus because you will eventually lesson to the devil in all situations. I have heard of classes called anger management classes. They are straight from the devil. There is no such thing as Anger management. The devil has our government teaching anger management. Jesus says to put off the sins of this world!!! Jesus tells us how to do it!

If you make a continuous effort to shut down the past memories of hurt and anger you can defeat the devil. If you forgive them for they know not what they do, you can be set free to think and dwell on the Jesus in you and the future you have with Him dwelling in you is more joy than we can comprehend! The truth of the word of Jesus sets us free from sin, death and anger. That is more Joyfulness then a perfect day at Kings Island could ever be. Praise God! Let's continue. Forgiveness is freedom and freedom is simply dwelling on the one who wants to dwell in you. JESUS!!!!!

If Jesus came right in this camper right now and sat down in front of you, could you think about your past or would you suddenly be in the joy of His presents. I guarantee you, you could not think about the past, or have anger or unforgiveness. You would be in such awe that all you could think about would be Him sitting there in front of you. Jesus is in front of you! Try to have anger with Jesus in front of you, looking at you, talking to you and wanting to spend time with you! Jesus said draw nigh to me and I will draw nigh to you. So ask Jesus to show you how to draw nigh to Him and He will be sitting in front of you and you can live in his presents every moment of your life. That is Joy to the MAX!!! That is freedom to the max. That is no more anger ever and that is no more past, it is future that is bright to the max!!! Jesus is the light of the world, and so are you when you are aware of the Jesus living in YOU!!!!

The devil came up with this thing called anger management, if you're trying to manage anger you are lessoning to the wrong

9

kingdom and you will never overcome the anger problem. Anger management is like trying to drive across a river with no bridge. You will sink and be in bed with anger that will chock you and snuff out your love of life. Stop anger in its tracks once and forever! Get born again, walk in the newness of your new blood line and talk to your new and real Father God. Come in to the truth that sets you free that is the relationship you can have with Jesus and your Father. Drive on the bridge of Hope and Live before God and I can tell you for a fact anger and the past will flee faster than a high speed bullet. Don't get in bed with anger, don't manage anger, just recognize it for what it is and kick it out by asking Jesus in to your life now, Today. That is freedom the bible talks about.

Talking about the past again and again will only reinforce the past. It keeps it up front in your mind and makes it hard to move on. So right now repeat after me. Jesus I am sorry about living in the past and letting the past rob me of my future. I today declare I will live for you and you alone. We have four wonderful children, your gifts to us and you must have known we can learn to seek you above all else and in that seeking you will be our peace and Joy that you have for us. We declare today Father that you are our Father and that makes us sons and daughters of the most high. We declare that we will live with you setting right in front of us because you dwell in us. Thank You Jesus, I love you too!!!

Jesus came to show us the Love of the Father and we will study Your word to learn how to live in that love and be that love to everyone on the earth. Jesus Thank You for your sacrifice that forever restored our relationship to you. We will take advantage of our relationship with You and live to talk to you and be with you living within us. Oh Father what better gift could you have given us then to be able to talk to you personally!!! You wanting a relationship with me is Peace and Joy and LOVE!!!! I truly need nothing else!!!

Sometimes people ask me how do you do this? How do you take care of Jenny 24/7? You never get time to do anything you want to do? I tell them I am the most blessed man on earth to have Jenny with me. I talked about living like Jesus was right in front of you all your life. Well Jenny is with me all my life. When I get upset about something I look over at Jenny and realize she is not upset. If I start to worry and then I see Jenny and she is not worried. Jenny takes no account of wrongs. Jenny doesn't even have to repent because she cannot sin. Jenny never brings up the past! I am blessed to live with someone that is so God like in so many ways, why would I need a break.

On the Contrary I want more of Jenny in my life. Seriously Jenny is a good influence on my life even in the situation we are in. I love my Jesus for the love He shows us every day and every minute. I thank you Jesus for setting such an example for us to follow. We all need truth and you are the truth that sets us free. Thank You for our freedom!!! Thank you Jesus for protection but most of all for your truth that sets us free from disease, sickness, and gives us health, joy and your perfect love!!!

November 11 2012 is our 40th anniversary and I am so full of joy. I really cannot tell if Jenny is excited but she is very alert and I praise my loving Father for our 40th together. After church this morning, I sat with Jenny on my lap and just held her. I talk a lot about not dwelling on the past, but today I did let my mind drift back on past anniversaries, although they were happy memories and full of joy, there was sadness also. Our children are all grown and doing their own thing. I started thinking about all the good anniversaries and eating in the dining room on Jenny's china. Our children always got excited when we ate in the dining room. Our anniversaries were always happy and thinking about them I could almost smell Jenny's cooking. I am so blessed to have such great memories of our anniversaries.

As I sat there with Jenny on my lap I started to get sad and I was looking at Jenny's little face as she was sleeping on my shoulder and I was wishing she would just wake up totally normal. The sadness started turning into regret and then some guilt came on me thinking maybe somehow I caused this. You know maybe there was some way I could have headed off the picks disease before it got this bad. Then all of a sudden I heard someone say to me, who is this guy you are listening to? Right away my countenance picked up and I knew I was letting myself go down the wrong path. Thank You Jesus and Father God for sending me a message through your Holy Spirit who dwells in me to get on with the day and not dwell on the past.

It was amazing to me how quickly the devil was turning the great memories of our anniversaries into sadness and then regret. We have been so blessed, I mean it, we are big time blessed! I love you Jesus and my heart and mind and my soul belong to you and You alone!!!!

The weather was unusually warm and Jenny woke up so I walked Jenny in the wheel chair. The campground was almost empty but Jenny and I enjoyed our walk even though we didn't talk to anyone. When we got back to our camper I decided to make Jenny's chocolate chip cookies. They taste great and I know they are oh so good for us! I love the smell of fresh cookies cooking in the oven and I think Jenny liked the smell also. I love my Jenny and I am so thankful to Jesus for giving me these very special times with His delightfully precious Jenny! You know this was the best anniversary ever!!!! Thank You Jesus for loving us so much!!

On the 18th we went to the church, where the 20 children invited us to. Oh I'm sorry I just jumped out in front of myself. Last weekend we met a group of 20 young teenagers from a church in Louisville. They were like sponges soaking up the word of Jesus. So I gave them all some tracks to read and they invited Jenny and I to their church. It was fun to see them again but they were in their own environment and so busy. They did talk to us but only briefly.

On Monday Jenny and I went to Louisville to have more books printed. On the way I ask Jesus if I should only have five printed because I knew I was running really close on my monthly budget. I got to Office Max and when the clerk ask me how many books do you want, ten came out of my mouth and so I just figured Jesus new something I didn't know.

Upon arriving home to our camper, a pickup truck pulled up. It was a lady we met at the church nearby (Family Christian Center). When she met us a week ago she realized Jenny was in depends and she explained how her work (a home for mentally challenged children and young adults) was acuminating extra depends. We literally stocked our camper in every place possible with pampers and bed pads. It was so nice of her to think of us and have the right size for Jenny. I mean I was over whelmed and just could not thank her enough.

Later Jenny and I went to pick up some groceries. At the checkout I looked at the bill surprised by the small amount. Then I realized I did not have pampers in the cart and that just saved me 24 dollars. Thank you Amy and Jesus for your thoughtfulness!!!! I look around the camper and see all these pamper and I feel soooo pampered. Jesus always comes through and He always does it by flowing through someone willing to be His representative here on earth. Thank you Amy and Thank You Jesus for taking care of my delightful precious Jenny! Thank you Amy for pampering us!

On Wednesday night Jenny and I went to church at the Family Christian Center. Pastor Pat has a great message and we have met a lot of very nice people there. He ended his message with announcements and asks his congregation if he missed anything. His wife said yes and then announced she knew of someone in the church who had a special need and ask the congregation to bless this family in their congregation. She didn't want to mention their name for fear they might be embarrassed. So they just placed a bucket at the exit.

A couple started talking to us as everyone else was leaving. They kept us occupied until almost everyone had left. Then a guy walked up and handed me a wade of cash and said the collection was for you and Jenny. They had no way of knowing our needs because I never expressed them but again Jesus put it in their hearts to give us a finical blessing. I usually do not talk about financial blessings because the blessings from God are always above them but there are some times when a bundle of cash is also needed and thanks to the special people of Pat's congregation Jenny and I are blessed again. I say again because the biggest blessing was being there with them. Thank you again Jesus!!!!

I could not believe what was happening in my heart. I mean Jesus had put love in the hearts of so many to bless us. I Thank You Jesus for your desire to bless Jenny and I! I Love You Jesus for letting us witness Your love flowing through so many others. I have been taught buy Jesus; how Jesus wants us to be Jesus on the earth; how Jesus wants us to love as Jesus loved on the earth.

13

I never quite understood why it was so important for Jesus to have us manifest Jesus. I mean Jesus did a great job of manifesting the Father's love! We can read about the love of Jesus in the bible, the ultimate love story. Now I am just starting to realize why Jesus wants us to manifest Him. The best way for Jesus to create a desire for people to want to know Him is to let people see Him in them. It is awesome; we can manifest Jesus by simple acts of kindness and in doing so we can give people a desire to know why we were kind.

I know some churches love to count the number of people that recite the sinner's prayer and get saved. They usually say "if you died to night where would spend eternity?" Then people recite the prayer and the church counts them as saved. That approach falls shot because their desire for Jesus came out of fear of going to hell! To me that is so short of the love of Jesus and they really have nothing to run on. I heard a preacher say "but what if they live tonight how did reciting the sinner's prayer help them live in everyday life?" I think when someone can witness the love of Jesus in you they will want what you have. They will have a desire to know Jesus and in that desire Jesus will fill them with truth and love that is the truth and love they see in you! Jesus said it is the love of Jesus that will lead men to repentance. Give the love of Jesus by being the love of Jesus and Jesus will bring the increase.

I think I know now why manifesting the love of the Father is so important. I think when we manifest YOU we get excited in our hearts and become very joyful in our hearts. This is the transforming of our minds YOU talk about in YOUR word. I guess Jesus gets so joyful in his heart to see his loved ones giving out of unconditional love; and watching joyfulness over flowing and spilling out of everyone in his church. I thank you Jesus for your love and for giving your life so willingly!! Jesus you are the best example of love this world has ever seen! I also thank you for your word, and the knowledge this world will be saved one heart at a time.

One heart at a time! Like a farmer plants seeds one seed at a time. I know tech knowledge has increased and so is the farmers speed at planting seed has increased but tech knowledge has also boosted are ability to plant seeds in the hearts of so many hearts at a time. A farmer plants a row at a time and a roe becomes a field and a field becomes an acre and the acres become a farm. Just as the farmer can feed thousands with his seeds planted in the ground, and he will never see all the people that benefit from his work, he knows in his heart the work is needed and necessary to sustain life. So to our seeds are planted to nourish the hearts of many and all though we usually never see the result of our labors; we can walk by faith knowing our labors are touching the hearts of many. Then every once in a while we will be given a powerful glance at the love of God flowing through others and how that love is the manifestation of our hearts for God's likeness. So never get discouraged, go plant some seeds of love and even if the people don't except them right away, rest in your belief that like the seed the farmer planted in the ground, will have a miracle of life in it and God will bring the increase.

I want to talk about me for a couple minutes. When I was only 5 or 6 years old I already loved little ones. Every year my Grandma had a party. We always called them Grandma's party. You would call them family reunions. Every year Grandma had a picture of her family taken. I was always in the front row sitting on the grass holding a baby in my lap. I was just fascinated with babies even at that early age. I loved the way they would look you in the eye and if you talked to them they would try to talk back. They watched your lips and your expressions to see if they made you happy. They would smile at you and coo at you and give you such joy. I truly love babies even when others made fun of me for holding and talking to babies, when I could have been playing games with children my own age.

I told you all that to say this. Right now Jenny is like the babies I have loved all my life. I sit on the couch and hold her in my lap like a baby and she looks right in my eyes and then studies my face expressions like the babies did. I talk to her and see her mouth try to move and I tell her she can talk to me. She tries so hard to talk and her little face makes expressions that blow my mind. I tell her I understand and smile at her, Jenny responds to love just like the babies did all my life. I tell people how God out does Himself every day. I tell them how I never knew of the joy

He could bring in to our life every day and I don't understand life, but I know I have the most blessed life of anyone I know!! THANK YOU JESUS for these truly special times with my loving little wife Jenny!!!

Thank you God for letting me hold Jenny in my arms and for letting me know when I am holding her, you are holding us, so we know you are present with us! As I write this I feel so inadequate to express the love of you Jesus but I know you understand because you told us your love would surpass all our understanding and IT DOES!!

December 1st, 2012

Last night I received a phone call Joel. We talked for over an hour and most of our conversation was about what a great guy I am. After we hung up I thought that is the third phone call this week where people told me I'm a good guy. Each phone call was a little different but pretty much the same. I ask God what is going on? Why do people all of a sudden think they need to tell me these things? I love you Father God and I think you are up to something. I guess I'll just wait and see. I thanked everyone for the kind words they spoke about me. I also praised my Father and brother Jesus because without them I really am so helpless to take care of my delightfully precious Jenny. What a gift she is and what a joy it is to have her here with me. Thank you Jesus for your words of encouragement!!! I love you too!!!

This morning as I was feeding Jenny, I was thanking God for Jenny being with me. I was praising Him for Jenny being able to swallow. I can tell Jenny's swallowing has become a big decision, it is not automatic like for most people. Smiling is the same way. Jenny has to work and think about getting her mussels in her face to smile. It seems that everything Jenny does is a contusions decision. I believe her life proves the love God has for her and His love is giving her the will power to still fight and because of the love from Jesus Jenny will not give up. She just needs massive amounts of love every day, and I know God and I are up for that. Thank you Jesus for your love every day!!!

Being in love with Jesus and knowing He loves us is so wonderful. Even being in this love relationship with Jesus, I see more negative things going on in Jenny's health then positive. It is very hard to witness; I mean I have the word of God that says He will heal all. I see the love of God every day, so I don't go by what

I see negatively, I go by Faith that God has turned this around and the three of us will have coffee together real soon.

1st Timothy 1:5 says the goal of our instruction is love from a pure heart and a good conscience and a sincere faith. I know Jesus showed everyone what love is and what a pure heart looks like, a good conscience, and a sincere faith looks like while here on earth. He is our example so I will seek Him for a pure heart of love and a good conscience and I will seek Him for a sincere faith that God has given me a desire for!!! I know Jenny already has hers and what an example she is! Again thank you Jesus for healing Jenny and thank you for your love and concern for our well-being. I love you Jesus!!!!

Last night I was holding Jenny on my lap and I started singing to her, about (you know who) my Father God. In my mind I saw a huge church; I'm using the word church because I have no other way to describe it. I guess I could call it a gathering place. I mean millions of spirits where there, the church was brilliant like nothing I have ever seen before, everyone was singing, here comes the bride, I have never heard music so beautiful before. There were no seats in this church, and no walls but I knew it was a holly place and everyone was just everywhere. The music was loud but soft somehow and very comforting, I did not see people playing music but I could hear it so clearly.

The song went like this (here comes the bride, here comes the bride and then someone else sung over their singing somehow and his voice sung; now all step aside as others continued singing here comes the bride) and then as everyone parted, like to form an aisle, I saw Father God walking down the aisle holding Jenny, not holding her hand like we do here on earth but holding her somehow like in His arms as you would hold a baby. Jenny looked so radiant!!! She was smiling with her little crocket tooth showing; as Father God presented her sinless and spotless and worthy to be the bride of His son Jesus. Believe me Joy is not a feeling in heaven it is a way of life!!! Peace is not achieved like here on earth, it is knowing you made it and you are in the presents of God himself!!!

Jesus said in his word that we are to be the bride of Jesus Christ and I know Jesus let me have this vision to give me the piece of Jesus Christ. I don't know when or how all that will work out but I know Jenny is the bride of Jesus and I get to witness the marriage!!! I will see Jesus with Jenny and as I am writing this I am hearing Jesus say (you ask Me if you will know Jenny in heaven or at least know that she is there.) My Jesus answers all questions and this time the answer is in a spectacular vision with beauty that is out of this world and singing that is so clear and so beautiful, my heart wants us to be their right now!!!

Something about that vision really stands out in my mind. Jenny's smile is the prettiest smile I have ever seen. She has a crooked tooth and although she never complained about it she did ask one time to have it fixed. One of the health insurance companies we had years ago had a dental plain included in it. Jenny asked if she could get her tooth fixed. I said if it is important to you go ahead, but I like your teeth just the way they are. I told Jenny I thought her crooked tooth gave her smile personality and complemented her very special face. I love her dimple on the left side of her face and the crocked tooth on the right side. Jenny has green eyes and that made her eyes special to me. I remember taking Jenny to a beauty parlor for a hair cut one time and the beautician ask to pluck Jenny's eyebrows? I said positively NO. I like Jenny's face just the way God made it! I love Jenny and I love her looks also. I love God for making Jenny so cute. Jenny's eye brows are just beautiful the way God made them. I know Jesus calls Jenny delightfully precious but He made her so cute; so beautifully cute. Thank You Jesus for making Jenny delightfully beautiful to me also and thank You for all these blessings!!!

Isn't it amazing that in the vision I could not tell it was Jenny coming down the aisle with Father God until I saw her smile? The other thing I liked about her smile was, Jenny was the only one with that smile. Jesus made Jenny so special to me! Jenny never asked about having her tooth fixed again. Thank You Jesus!

When I told some people about this vision their comment was; Jesus is preparing you for when Jenny goes to be with the Lord. I could see how they could think that. I asked Jesus if He was preparing me to be comforted here on earth without Jenny. I believe Jesus was just answering my question about will I know

Jenny made it and will I see her there. Jesus saw my concern and loves me so much He decided to quite my heart by giving me a beautiful vision of heaven and Jenny being very Joyful there. In a way he let me know that he likes Jenny's crooked tooth and her delightfully precious special smile. I love You Jesus and I thank You for Your very special way of loving us!!! You know Jesus you are delightfully precious to Jenny and I !!!!!!

Before I had that little vision of heaven I had been asking Jesus if I would know Jenny in heaven? It seemed important to me, I cannot figure out how you could love someone so much and then get to heaven and not want to be married their also. I know the bible stories that talk about heaven and the word heaven is mentioned 583 times and in 551 verses in the bible, and of those 256 times and 238 verses are in the New Testament. So I guess it is important to God for us to know we have a place to go. The very first scripture verse mentions heaven.

Gen 1:1 In the beginning God created the heaven and the earth.

Jesus created it and I want to go. Thank You God for that special vision and for telling us about the reward of going to heaven, to be with You and our loved ones!!!

In a conversation with a friend I met the through Joel; Christopher explained to me how knowing God is not enough. He said everyone knows the president of the United States. You could study the president and read every book he has ever written, you could get to know him so well, you could know what he had for breakfast every day. If you had all this knowledge and then you went to the white house and ask to see the president, all that knowledge, all the studying, and all the research you did would still not get you in to see the president. The only way to be invited in is for the president to know you. Christopher said I believe God is the same way. He said you can study God and research God and have great knowledge of God; you can quote bible scriptures all day and still not have a relationship with God.

I thought to myself, God is not limited in knowledge like the president and God knows us all, I mean God created us all, so wouldn't God let us in? The answer is the same, you could know everything about the president or God but if you have no relationship, all that knowledge is useless!!! Kind of like knowing

20

someone who can quote the bible, verse for verse but he never lives in the Joy of knowing Jesus wants a heart to heart, loving relationship with him. He has missed the real reason Jesus came!!!

I decided to ask God. How do we become more intimate with you Jesus? I already have a good relationship with you but just like my relationship with Jenny grew over the years I want to continue to grow a more personal intimate, lasting, loving relationship with You Jesus. Jesus answered with a question. How could it be that someone could be a neighbor of yours and after twenty years of living next door to you, one day the police pull up and arrest him for being a serial killer? You are totally surprised because you never had the slightest idea your neighbor was a serial killer. Jesus said your problem is, you never really talked to your neighbor and more importantly you never lessened to him either. Jesus said you never made knowing him your priority and you never sought a relationship with him! Jesus said you were content to know he did not bother you and you did not bother him. You only gained enough knowledge to be comfortable. He said you were comfortable just knowing his name and most of all you were comfortable thinking you were safe having him for a neighbor, so you did not need any more knowledge of him except to be comfortable having him next door.

I have found in my travels that comfort brings complaisance, you see I love to talk about God to everyone I meet and I do talk about God to everyone, but when I have been around someone long enough I get comfortable knowing they have a relationship with Jesus and then we start talking about other things because we become comfortable around each other.

I thought to myself, Jesus you are so right! Most people have been taught the only reason Jesus came was to dye for our sins; we pray a little prayer and we are saved. They never seek a heart to heart relationship with Him. This would be like me marring someone because I like the way she makes pancakes. She may think this is easy, all I have to do is make him pancakes every day and he will take care of me. You may have loved her pancakes for a while but after a few months of pancakes you might want something different. If your relationship with God is based on something so superficial, like what Has God promised you, the first time you do not get what you think he has promised, you will think why is this happening or worse you may ask, why did you let that happen God?

Your relationship probably will not last. You will probably backslide or get divorced because your relationship was based on the superficial knowledge, of thinking I'll pray this little prayer and God is now my provider. You never grew your relationship to know Him better! You never ask God what do you want me to do today! Love is a two way street. Love is responding to the needs of your loved one every day. Don't just tell God you love Him, be His love to all you met today and every day and you will prove you Love Jesus.

The first step to a good relationship is lessoning! The second is responding to what you heard. I mean we want Jesus to lesson to us and to respond to us, don't we? Jesus is lessoning and responding all the time. We need to do the same! When you hear His voice and respond you are doing the will of the Father and doing the will of the Father will bring Joy to you that can and will flow through you to others. It really is a Joy that surpasses our understanding because you and Jesus are building a relationship that will last forever.

If you lesson to your bride and you respond to her, you will have a great relationship and if you live to learn more about her every day your love and understanding will grow every day!!! Jesus is the Bride, start each day by asking Him; Jesus what are we going to do today!!! Then go about your day and watch God put a circumstance in your path to share the love of Jesus to someone. It never fails and it is Joy beyond your understanding!! Never just tell someone about God, give them the love of God!!! Be willing to be the representative of God's love and watch God's love change hearts one at a time. Jesus said my burden is light and my yoke is easy and as you know He is sooooo right! Go give someone the love of Jesus to day. Please don't try to give someone the love of Jesus to feel loved by God that is backwards, give them the love of Jesus because you know you are loved by Jesus! When you know and are rooted in the love of Jesus, loving others will be as easy as

December 8th, 2012

We moved to Lebanon, Ohio to be closer to Mom and our boys for the season. Jesus had me finish the teaching on Hero's and I had copies made so I could start handing them out. On Thursday while passing through Red Lion, Ohio we stopped for a haircut at a barber shop I saw there. I could tell Steve the barber had a big heart the moment I walked in, because he wanted to make sure Jenny was comfortable while he cut my hair. As we talked about God another guy came and we soon had a three-way conversation going. After finishing my hair cut I went out to the car to get them both a copy of Coffee Time. I handed them both a copy of coffee time when another guy came in. We continued talking about God when the third fellow said "I used to do nice Christian things for people but they never thank you so I stopped doing them".

I just stood there thinking; Lord how do I respond to that? Just then Jesus whispered in my ear, give him the teaching on heroes, so I looked at him and said I have something you might like to read. Then I went to the car again and got a copy for him. As I reentered the barbershop the three of them were laughing, the man getting his hair cut had started reading Coffee Time and had gotten to the part where Jenny flipped me the bird. He said your little wife must have been a real flip. I told them she was. I handed the teaching on heroes to the sarcastic man and shortly after that Jenny and I left.

On the following Monday I was talking to Steve the barber from Red Lion barber shop on the phone, he was excited to tell me what happened after I left Thursday. The barbershop is on a busy street with a traffic light in front of it. Steve said the three of them were sill talking about Coffee time with Jesus, when they herd a woman screaming for help. They ran outside and saw a county bus had stopped at the red light and the woman driver was outside the buss trying to hold the door shut as a man inside the bus was trying to kick the door open. The bus was a special buss for the mentally challenged and this man had broken out of his restraints and started attacking the driver. The three men from the barbershop manned the doors of the bus, while someone called 911.

The sarcastic man from the barbershop jumped in the buss with the wild man and talked the wild man into trading the ballpoint pen the wild man was attacking him with, for a role of tape. In moments he had the man settled down and when the police came they secured him in his seat and all was well again. The three men went into the barbershop and Steve told the sarcastic man, I could not have done what you did, getting into that buss with the wild man. Steve said that was really heroic! The man looked at Steve and started laughing and then said you know the man with his wife that was here a little while ago gave me a paper to read. Steve said yes what was it? The paper is titled HERO'S. All three men had a good laugh and said what a day this has been.

A couple days' later Jenny and I went to see Mom. We had a nice visit. Mom is now off some of her medicine and she is so much more alert then in past visits. It was really good to see her and I gave her a new copy of Jenny's book. This one has about 30 more pages then the first one I gave her.

This Christmas season was different from last year. Last year it seemed Jenny and I had someone to visit every night. This year we spent a lot of time in the camper but it turned out really cool because Joel had time to come over and we meet some of his friends that came over with their three children. Also one night we were invited to Will Riddles house where we met three young men that were from Russia. Jenny and I had a great time there and the whole night went so fast. Everyone there was on fire for the Lord and their fire made my fire even hotter. It was a special time to say the least. I love you Jesus for putting friends in our life that build our relationship with You. Thank you Will and Jamie for having us over, what a special time that was.

On another night we went to Mary and Kerns house for a great dinner. We also had great conversation. Their son Sam read the Heroes paper and said he liked the part about Mc Donald's. Their daughter Libby read it and said she liked it also. I was glade Mary and Kern and children had time to visit with us because I love spending time with them.

One night Joel showed me how to e-mail. So I e-mailed a copy of Jenny's book to Will and he formatted it for me and sent the book to Amazon to have it published. He did it so fast that I had 10 copies before Christmas. Thank you Will, you are amazing. He wanted to have the book edited but I said it is not about having a perfect book, more importantly it is about getting what God is doing through Jenny out in the world and to have an impact in the world. Jenny's first book is in print and to me that was a big deal. Thank you Will and Thank you paying for them also. You have made this a very special Christmas for Jenny and I!

December 12th, 2013

Around the 12th we received a phone call from Bob, a friend who said he had about a two hour window of time and if we could make it to Bob Evans he would buy us lunch. Jenny and I made it there and met our friend. Before we ordered our food, Bob told me how his wife asked him a question before she left for work that morning. She wanted to know if she were to get sick like Jenny; could he take care of her like Ron takes care of Jenny? All during our meal Bob was analyzing himself and had decided he could take care of his wife like I do except he could not carry her around the way I carry Jenny. Bob said he would have to use the wheel chair more than I do, but other than that he was quite sure he could take care of his wife if she became sick like Jenny.

We were almost finished eating when Jenny's bowels let loose. I told Bob I was going to take Jenny to the restroom to clean her up. We were so blessed to have the restroom empty and none of the mess got on the floor as I carried Jenny into the restroom. It was quite a mess. The depends did not hold and the mess went down her legs and into her socks. The toilet did not have a toilet tank; it just had the chrome pipe and flush valve. That makes it very hard to keep Jenny from falling while I am trying to clean her. I used a lot of wipes and managed to do a good job. I got a clean out fit on Jenny and as I picked her up her bowel let loose again. I really felt bad for Jenny, I mean we share all our meals and my bowels were just fine. I'm not sure what I gave her to have her bowels like mud. The good news is she didn't seem to be in any pain.

I started to clean Jenny up again. The partitions in public restrooms are about a foot of the floor. When a man came in to use the urinal I heard him say whoo as the smell was horrible and you could see the dirty pampers and wipes laying on the floor. I did not open the door of the stall but I ask him if he could find Bob out in the restaurant. I described Bob to him and the man found Bob. Bob came in and could see the mess under the partition. He asked me what I needed. I told him I had another clean outfit for Jenny in the back seat of our car and needed him to get it for us. He went and got the clean clothes and handed them over the partition to me.

I got Jenny dressed and out to the car. After I buckled her in the seat I then ran back in to Bob Evans to clean the restroom and put the messy depends and wipes in the garbage can. When I finished in there I gathered up Jenny's soiled clothes and headed out to say good bye to Bob, who was waiting by Jenny. Bob had kind of a sick look on his face and said Ron, I don't think I could do this. He hugged me and said I think you are pretty special Ron. I thanked Bob for lunch and he handed me a Christmas card with some cash in it. I thanked him and he left. It was really nice to have some extra cash and I know how hard Bob and Barb work for their money. It is deeply appreciated. Thank you Jesus for friends like Bob and Barb.

I went back in to the restaurant to ask the manager to have someone change the bag in the garbage can or the stink will continue on. A young man went in to change the bag; I went right in the restroom after him to ask him if he wanted me to change it. It is a little messy I said. He told me he would do it and added thanks for cleaning the mess up so good. He then asked me what happened to your wife. I gave him the short version because I really needed to get Jenny home to shower her and do the laundry. It was nice of that young man to ask about my Jenny. Thank you Jesus for putting such nice people in our path everywhere we go!!

December 16th, 2013

I know we went to see mom again around the 16 of December and had another nice visit. Mom is so much more alert then last year and that makes my Christmas great already and just seeing her be her old self again is such a blessing. We were there a couple hours when mom leaned over and whispered something to my brother Kenny. Kenny told me mom said I'm tired when are they leaving? I just loved seeing mom drinking her coffee and seeing her walk to the bathroom, it was a special visit for Jenny and I; but the night was over and off we went. Thank You Jesus for a wonderful visit with mom!!! Jenny and I had sat on moms couch that whole time and I was amazed how well Jenny seemed to be lessoning.

The weather has been really cold for the last couple days, so Jenny and I have had a lot of time in the camper. Jenny really doesn't seem to be concerned about not going anywhere so I have pretty much just been holding her and loving on Jenny all day long. Even when I go do the laundry Jenny seems to understand. I think she is doing really good. Praise my Jesus and praise you some more.

On the 19th of December we received a call from Marilyn my sister, she told me mom had taken a turn for the worse and I needed to come over to see her. We did go and what a difference a couple days make. Hospice was there and just making mom comfortable, it was really hard to see mom like that but what a blessing for us to already be in Cincinnati and close by. All her children were there except Elaine who lives in California.

We went back to see mom the next day. The nurses said she was now totally unresponsive. I leaned over her bed and said

Jenny and I came to see you Mom, the nurses were right, there was no response at all. So I leaned over her bed again and said Mom it is Ronnie the one that shook your China closet when I was bad. Mom started to laugh, the nurses sprang to their feet to see her response and mom just got a big smile on her face. God blessed me with that smile and I will hold onto that smile the rest of my life. Thank you Jesus for being so thoughtful as to give me what turned out to be mom's last smile!

On Friday the 21st of December mom passed on to spend eternity with Jesus and Father God. I believe Jesus sent her a special invitation to spend Christmas with Him and His Father and mom said I'll be there and she was. I'm so happy for her and I know her work her on earth was complete; so her death was the right timing of my Jesus and what a comfort to know mom is up there with Jesus. I know most of the time we humans think of death from the perspective of our loss. If you look at death form the perspective of life in heaven with Jesus it gives a whole new outlook on death and death can be celebrated for what is (a reward form God for a job well done.) Just thinking about Mom being in heaven is such a great joy for me! Thank You Jesus.

A couple weeks ago we were invited to have dinner and spend the evening with Doug and Ann, on December 22nd. We have been friends for over 45 years. Our dinner was great and as the night unfolded Doug ask if I had a sport jacket to where to mom's funeral. Doug gave me a really nice jacket and a dress shirt. It looked brand new and fit perfect. It was really nice of Doug and Ann to invite us over for dinner and we had a great time enjoying their company. Now I knew I could go to mom's funeral and look great for her, because Doug's sport coat did fit and looked great. What a nice thing for Doug and Ann to do and what a great time Jenny and I had visiting them. I am over whelmed at the timing of my Jesus. He planned this dinner with Doug and Ann a couple weeks ago. Then God put it in the hearts of Doug and Ann to give me dress clothes for Mom's funeral. I would never spend the money to buy dress clothes for one event and yet God cared enough to gift them to me. Jesus you are the best!!!

We spent Christmas day with Robbie and Sue, my nephew and his wife along with their three children. We all went to Sue's, sister's house for a great Christmas. They are so much fun to be around. I thought it is so cool to see a family get along so well. Sue received a warm blanket from her sister that said "my sister has the greatest sister in the world" I think they are great people and for Jenny and I it was great to share the Joy of Christmas with such joyful people. Jenny and I are blessed to see them all again.

On Friday the 28th of December mom's body was laid at the Gate of Heaven cemetery next to Dad's grave site. The reality of it has not really set in but I know they are with my Jesus and my Father God so I have a great Joy in my heart knowing they are loved and spending eternity in heaven. Now mom and dad are in the peace and joy the Lord talked about all the time! Thank you Jesus.

During the week between Mom's death and her Funeral Jesus gave me a teaching on inheritances. It was 12 pages long and I hoped to read it at mom's Mass. I thought it was very important but I did not get the opportunity to read it. I did get to hand it out to some of the people there. Jesus said Inheritance should not be material junk, inheritance should be passing on the knowledge of knowing God and passing that knowledge to your children. Anything other than His knowledge to pass on is junk that actually might take you further from God instead of growing you closer to Him.

I know some people would disagree and call the junk "keep sakes" but what are the keep sakes keeping and what are they making you dwell on. If not God then I don't need it. For example if you think you own something and that something would be hard to give up, you don't own it, it owns you. To me keep sakes are like that. You try to hold on to them and in reality they are holding on to you. Let go of the Junk and live to love and be the love of Jesus in the world! Now that is true freedom and you can hand that down to everyone and you do not need lawyers or wills!

I am free to be who God wants me to be and I do not need junk to tie me down. I told my brothers and sisters to do what they want with mom and dads "keep sakes". I love my brothers and sisters and respect their desire for those things but I am just interested in doing the work of the kingdom of God. Having the love of Jesus in my heart and knowing He loves me is the greatest keepsake in the world and the only one that will see us through life's hardships!!!

When I think about heaven I know the coolest part will be being with Father God and Jesus!!! I think just seeing them and knowing you made it will be joy beyond anything we can imagine here on earth. I believe in heaven we will have enough. Enough of what you might ask? Enough of everything. You see here on earth we consume so much of our time trying to have enough. Like money or food or whatever you think you might need.

I know Jesus told us not to worry, but people do. Jesus tells to take no thought for tomorrow, but people do. Actually we worry so much about tomorrow we lose our Joy for today. Then tomorrow comes and we start worrying about the next tomorrow. I believe we can be in heaven right now if we stop worrying. Jenny and I just trust God to provide and He does! Tomorrow is not promised to anyone and the things we worry about today are projected on to tomorrow. It is a useless cycle. Life is simple TRUST GOD and rest in His love and forget trying to hold on to Physical Keep Sakes! I know for a fact that mom loved me so what else do I need from her.

Next I'd like to share what Jesus and I wrote for mom's funnel.

YOUR INHERITANCE

12/22/12

The day after Mom's death while having coffee time with Jesus, He started talking about comfort zones. How stepping out of a comfort zone will make you grow in the Lord. Leaving a comfort zone is like stepping in to the unknown. Like the first day of school for a child, he is leaving the comfort of home and going into the unknown. This transition will be a lot easier for him if his mom removes the fear by guiding him and assuring him it will be okay. After a short amount of time his fear leaves and he is comfortable there also. The reward for facing the fear is new knowledge and a bigger world.

For mom her comfort zone was her family and her familiar surroundings. Fear will hold you in a comfort zone until someone helps you remove the fear. It is like crossing a bridge, only we never know how long the bridge is or what awaits us on the other side. I believe Jesus sent a comforter for mom and took her to the final reward, of being with Jesus and Father God and a new world without fear.

I believe life is about preparing and helping others prepare for meeting our creator. On Friday December 21st 2012 at 9:30 pm mom crossed her last bridge. I thank Jesus for allowing mom to be in her comfort zone right up to her entrance into her eternal life. Mom was truly blessed to have almost all her loved ones alongside her. I believe mom had the peace of mind, knowing her loved ones were at piece; with her going to be with Jesus. When we cross the bridge in faith Jesus brings us to a new level of comfort. Jesus through His example is preparing us for the big bridges in life and Jesus comforts us with His love. Thank You Jesus for loving Mom and for being her loving guide in this transition. I like to think of mom's passing this way, Jesus just gave

32

mom an invitation to spend Christmas in heaven with Him and all His loved ones and mom said yes!

The life of Jesus is our example of how to live and how to love. Jesus uses the bible as a tool to teach us and we have a free will to decide if we want to follow Jesus on the narrow path or walk the path of destruction while thinking it is our own path. Either way we all get to cross the bridge and stand before Jesus for judgment. If we prepare for our judgment the judgment seat will be sweet and we will be in the loving arms of Jesus.

I know mom has crossed the bridge and is in heaven with Jesus. Today I pray for everyone here to be on the narrow path that Jesus talks about and for all of us to see the narrow gate and that it is open wide for us. I know Friday night my mom stood before Jesus and was judged. I believe her judgment was sweet and she is in the loving arms of Jesus and the Father! Actually I kind of envy her when I think of the Joy in her spirit! Mom is finally able to be with Jesus and Father God. Jesus said in Mathew;

> Mat 7:13-14 Enter ye in at the strait gate: for wide is the gate, and broad is the way, that leadeth to destruction, and many there be which go in there at: Because strait is the gate, and narrow is the way, which leadeth unto life, and few there be that find it.

So we see by God's word that strait is the gate and narrow is the way that leads unto life and only a few will find it. I believe mom and dad walked the narrow path and went through that gate. How do you find the narrow path? Simply put; you have childlike faith in God. I believe mom had that childlike faith. I believe mom never gave up on God. Even when her prayers were not answered as fast as she would have liked; mom stood steadfast in her believe that Jesus would answer them.

In other words we choose the path. The wide path is full of earthly goods and some happiness. Contrast that with the narrow path, little earthly goods, but full of Joyfulness. In my quite time with Jesus, He explained to me the difference between happiness and Joyfulness. Jesus said happiness is the devils counterfeit of Joyfulness. Jesus showed me happiness is living for yourself, and Joyfulness is denying yourself and living for others.

Happiness comes by someone doing something for you, it is momentary, it can come and go in seconds; we actually make plans

33

to be happy. We can plane to go to Kings Island and on that day have perfect weather, no long lines, great food, and when we go to our car to leave, if the car doesn't start we lose all our happiness in one second.

Contrast the happiness of living for yourself with the joy of living for others. Joyfulness is you doing something for others; it is forever and stays with you even in your times of need. Choosing to help others is choosing the narrow path and in doing so receiving the Joyfulness that will surpass our understanding. It is bring heaven to earth as Jesus spoke about in the prayer we call the "Our Father".

Jesus commanded us to die to self. I know mom died to herself all her life. Mom would give of her time to anyone that ask!

Luk 9:23 And he said to them all, If any man will come after me, let him deny himself, and take up his cross daily, and follow me.

I know there is a spiritual war going on for your spirit 24/7. The only way to win this war is to recognize you are in it. Yes,

First you must recognize that our battle is in the spirit world and our battle is for our eternal life and this spiritual battle will determine where you will spend eternality.

Eph 6:12 For we wrestle not against flesh and blood, but against principalities, against powers, against the rulers of the darkness of this world, against spiritual wickedness in high places.

For we wrestle not against flesh and blood. Flesh is material that can and will rote away. Blood is trying to pass on these material things on to loved ones. I believe material treasures are the curses of modern day. I have seen people work so hard to have something to hand their children when they die. People write wills so the children will not fight over their inheritance. I believe this is the (worrying about tomorrow) the bible talks about not doing. I met a couple that thought they simplified life by only having one child, only to see her go into drugs and an alternative life style. Then the parents had no one to leave their junk to.

My parents left us children an inheritance of material things. I believe there motive was pure and they just saw these things as keepsakes. I can tell you this; Jesus gave me the best inheritance anyone can ask for. The day before mom died when Jenny and I went to see her. As I entered her bedroom the hospice nurse said your mom has not recognized anyone today. I thought to myself, mom doesn't have her hearing aid in and she doesn't have her glasses on, so maybe she cannot hear us or see us and it may be hard for mom to talk.

I leaned over her bed and said it is Jenny and Ron here to see you mom. There was no response, just then I looked at mom and leaned over her again and said I'm Ronnie the one that shuck your china closet and mom smiled and tried to laugh. The nurses came to their feet as they were really surprised by mom's reaction. I know the next day I called to see how mom was doing and my sister Pat answered the phone. She said I heard you got mom smiling yesterday. I didn't realize it then, but I think it might have been her last smile. Thank you Jesus for the best inheritance anyone could ask for!!

I am so blessed to find the truth. Jesus said our fight is against principalities, against powers, against the rulers of the darkness of this world, against spiritual wickedness in high places. Principalities are devils, rulers of darkness are devils, spiritual wickedness is lessoning to devils and doing what they say. Today we could say our fight is against the principality of business, notice the word sin in the middle of bu-sin-ess. Our fight is always against time and against the sucking power of material. Material things do suck the life right out of you. We work hard to get them, to keep them nice, to preserve them, to keep them clean and we worry about who gets our junk when we leave this world. Sounds like false idols to me. As I walk closer to the Lord I realize anything that takes my mind off Jesus can be a false idol.

Look how hard we will work to have something nice. Look how many hours and days; we will give up with our loved ones to supply them with the right clothes and material things. While we are out working so hard for our children, the "Rulers of darkness" that is the evil spirits come in to steel our loved ones. When these evil spirits still our loved ones, we do not understand, I mean we worked so hard for our children. If we give them the chance to defend themselves, they will say all we wanted was for you to spend time with us dad. I know now I would have loved more then any material thing on earth to have more time with mom and dad. I kept thinking tomorrow or next week I'll have time and that tomorrow and next week never came. New cars, second home, season pass to see the bangles, all fall short of just having time to be with and talk to my mom and dad. Most people know you can talk to God anytime, so they put off talking to God also. I have learned that intimacy with Jesus brings more Joy then anything material could ever bring. I used to like movies but now to watch a two hour movie is wasting 120 minutes I could be spending with my best friend Jesus!

So how did mom and dad overcome all the material things of the world? They found the truth of Gods word.

Joh 8:32 And ye shall know the truth, and the truth shall make you free.

The truth is we should have our hearts seeking God. We should be telling our children to seek God and His joyfulness, by putting the needs of God first in life. (Denying self) The inheritance we can pass on to our children is the truth of God's word. We can do this without involving lawyers, wills and government regulations. We are free from all that. The inheritance should be such, that no one can still, kill and destroy it. The real inheritance to pass on to our children is a relationship to Jesus that sets us free of the world and all it has to offer.

The inheritance we should pass along is the truth of knowing Jesus loves us and we are the sons and daughters of Father God. The Freedom and truth Jesus is talking about is knowing material things no longer hold us in bondage, it is knowing we will never die! Our spirit is alive in us now and forever. While here on earth we can choose to follow Jesus and walk in the love of Jesus and have Heaven as a reward, that is true freedom. Or we can live in bondage to material junk, we can choose to love the world, love material things and have hell as a reward! When I say bondage I', talking about worry, worrying about money, bills, estates, who gets what, if your worrying about anything, that thing owns you, you don't own it.

You can choose to hug a tree, work until you cannot work anymore, save for a rainy day, work to pay life insurance, leave enough junk for your children to fight over! Supply them with all the material things you can and pray the fight for your junk doesn't start before you die, because it can.

Instead recognize your true treasure is intimacy with Jesus and you share Jesus with your children and neighbors! Approach them with a pure heart, instill in them your love of God and your freedom from sin! Instill in them the love and trust of the one who said (I will never leave you or forsake you). Knowing Jesus said in

Hebrews 13:5 I will never leave you or forsake you is freedom from the bondage of fear and the fear of loosing your junk.

Spend time with your treasures, talk to Jesus and your children, your neighbors and your loved ones and instill in them the love of Jesus. It might seem awkward at first but be truthful, tell them and show them how important they are to you. Read about the life of Jesus and share his love. Share the life of Jesus, be the life of Jesus and love like Jesus loved unconditionally. That is true freedom and when you get to the end of your life you will not need a will or layers because the inheritance you give your children is all ready in their heart.

I know for sure eternity is a long time. We can give so much of our life to acquiring earthly material, to being successful, to learning how to play the game here on earth and to acquiring college degrees, and in doing so forget to prepare for life eternal, we will impress everyone here with our knowledge and our junk, except the one who really cares, JESUS, and our loved ones. Remember happiness is the counterfeit of JOY. If what you are seeking only brings momentary happiness, it is not JOY. Bring Glory to God by choosing Him over the junk of the world is freedom and joyfulness. Choose God not junk! Why would I want to watch a movie or work for more junk when I could spend time talking to my best friend Jesus and my loved ones?

I know my mom and dad are in heaven and that brings me great Joy. I know I am having the time of my life right now every day because I don't look to my circumstances to bring me happiness I look to the true love of God and in doing so I know the joyfulness and freedom of a life without junk can bring. I know for a fact that God loves me. I am in true freedom from the world because I am secure in the love of Jesus. I do not need any

37

material things and my life is full of Joy because material things no longer hold me bondage. I don't wake up worrying about payments, insurance, bills, degrees or wanting of anything. I wake up and ask God what are we going to do today. My life is surrendered to God and I know God will do great things through me today. Jesus is the truth that sets us free form the bondage of material JUNK.

Life is simple, it is childlike faith. Seek God with all your heart and you will find the love of your life waiting and wanting to spend time with you! Just talk to Jesus like He is your best friend, because He is!!!! Jesus told me the way to have a great relationship is to lesson, that's right just lesson. Jesus said

> Joh 10:27-28 My sheep hear my voice, and I know them, and they follow me: And I give unto them eternal life; and they shall never perish, neither shall any man pluck them out of my hand.

Yes read and study the life of Jesus but most of all seek that personal relationship. Jesus said my sheep know my voice. How will you know His voice if we are to busy to lesson? How will we follow Him if we don't know Him? Jesus said seek and you will find! When you do, Jesus promises us eternal life!!

> Mat 7:7 Ask, and it shall be given you; seek, and ye shall find; knock, and it shall be opened unto you:

Ask God for relationship and it shall be given to you. Seek the truth of God's word and you will find, knock on the narrow gate and Jesus will open it unto you.

My brothers and sisters and all our loved ones here today, I ask for you all to just seek a relationship with Jesus. In doing so you will have joy in your life, peace that surpasses all understanding in your heart, the cleansing of forgiveness which is freedom foreveryone you know, and freedom form yourself. Knowing Jesus loves you will make you free from yourself. No one can hurt you when you live for others, because what they do or don't do; what they say or don't say is not going to make or break your day because the truth is YOU KNOW Jesus loves you. Knowing Jesus loves you is the truth that sets you free! People cannot hurt me because I don't live for their approval I already have the love of Jesus in my heart. I live to love others as Jesus loves them. I would like nothing more than to see all my loved ones know the truth that sets us free! I love Jesus but more important than that I know Jesus loves me!!! I AM FREE!!!!

Jesus wants intimacy with you. Your relationship with him can grow to where you can ask Him anything and receive an answer. For example; one morning while having coffee with Jesus I ask (Jesus I always describe Jenny as precious, how do you describe her? Immediately I heard the words delightfully precious.) I rejoice knowing my best friend and brother Jesus calls my wife "delightfully precious". You too can have this intimacy with God, in fact the real reason God sent His son was to restore the intimacy with us. Forgiving sin was a small part of why Jesus came.

Notice in John 10:27 it also says "and I know them"

Jesus loves me and I know it! Jenny and I will see Jesus and Father God and mom and dad someday. Your relationship with God is not just you knowing God, but rather you knowing that God knows you.

You could know everything there is to know about president Obama; you could study his life; you could know what he had for breakfast today, and if you went to see him at the white house they would not let you in to see him. All that knowledge would not gain you entrance to visit him. But if president Obama knows you; you will get right in. It is not enough for you to know of God, you must have intimacy with Him and to do that you must know His voice and he has to hear your voice, so the two of you can become one.

Jesus rejoices over us with singing. Yes Jesus sings over us like a mother holding a little one in her arms, or when parents rejoice seeing their children make good decisions.

Zep 3:17 The LORD thy God in the midst of thee is mighty; he will save, he will rejoice over thee with joy; he will rest in his love, he will joy over thee with singing.

Jesus will even reveal the song he sings over you if you ask and lesson for his voice.

Life eternal is not having a passport to heaven; it is having a relationship with Jesus and Father God and the Holy Spirit NOW! Here on earth! Jesus didn't just come to forgive us our sins. I am not just a sinner saved by grace; I am a son of God, I can talk to

39

my Father through Jesus 24/7 and I do. The Joy of the Lord is ours just for seeking a relationship with the one who has already laid down His life for us! Please don't read His word to see if it is true in your life, Read His word believing it is true in your life, and it will become true in your life. The best things in life are free because Jesus paid the price for me!

Please spend time with your best friend, seek Him with your whole heart, mind and soul. Teach your children to do the same and you will never worry about death, in fact you will rejoice in it. Your inheritance is in your heart!

Mom and Dad are in heaven! THANK YOU JESUS!!!!!

Mom and Dad are in the comfort of Jesus!!!! I know they know what it is to be free! I know Jesus is love and God the Father is love and the Holy Spirit is love, I know the comfort of Jenny's love (unconditional love) is the most in creditable love we can experience her on earth. I believe Jesus when he said you can accomplish in creditable things on earth but if they were done without love, you have not accomplished anything. When Jesus was talking about the commandments; Jesus said the greatest of these is love. Life is simple, read the life of Jesus and live as Jesus lived, He is our example! I have never read in the bible where Jesus said the words I love you, but I know He does by what He did. Love is not saying I Love you, love is being love every day in every way! Love is being Jesus!!!!

> Mat 5:43-48 Ye have heard that it hath been said, Thou shalt love thy neighbor, and hate thine enemy. But I say unto you, Love your enemies, bless them that curse you, do good to them that hate you, and pray for them which despitefully use you, and persecute you; That ye may be the children of your Father which is in heaven: for he maketh his sun to rise on the evil and on the good, and sendeth rain on the just and on the unjust. For if ye love them which love you, what reward have ye? do not even the publicans the same? And if ye salute your brethren only, what do ye more than others? do not even the publicans so? Be ye therefore perfect, even as your Father which is in heaven is perfect.

Yes we can be perfect for Jesus said so. Just be the love of God here on earth and God will make you perfect in His love!

Jenny and Jesus and I love you all forever!!

2013

Wow it is 2013 already. Jesus already gave me a new teaching this year called Fruits. It has a real cool story in it about trusting each other. I am going to post it on my web site coffee time with Jesus@yahoo.com.

We left Cincinnati for Carrolton Ky. We went to the Family Christian Center for church service and were able to give the pastor's wife a copy of Jenny's Wheel Chair. The people are so loving towards us and you can see the love of Jesus in there eyes as you talk with them. Kim met with us again and restocked us with pampers again. I have packed every nook and cranny of the motor home with pampers and pads. I feel so honored and blessed. Truly Jenny and I are so blessed to have this supply of pampers. Thank you Jesus for putting your love in the hearts of the people of the Family Christian Center and for their heart for Jesus! It is truly amazing to see your love flowing and to let us be part of your world Jesus.

My Jenny is doing pretty good. She has been sitting up and not stiffing out as bad as before. Her eyes are open a lot more and I believe she is responding better. Her swallowing is better also. Things can change from day to day. Like yesterday Jenny didn't eat hardly at all. Today though she will probably eat better again. If I go by my circumstances I would be on a roller coaster ride every day of my life for I don't know how many years. I just stay steadfast in the love God has for Jenny and I and I do not in any way lean on my own understanding.

If we could understand everything we would not need God, faith, or hope! If you do not believe me just look at the really smart people who think there is no God. They have no faith, hope and don't believe in God! They believe in their own understanding, which makes them their own God. Hitler was really smart and thought he was God. He thought he could create a perfect race by killing all the people that did not believe the way he did. His life didn't turn out to good. I guess you could say leaning on his own understanding did not work out to good for him. I hope he was smart enough to ask for forgiveness before he died.

I want to thank you Jesus for letting me see your love in the world. I want to thank you Jesus for the blessings of Love Faith, Hope, Trust and wisdom! The wisdom to know I do not need to know or understand everything. Thank you for the wisdom to know your word is sufficient, Your love is more than enough, and you give us hope beyond our reasoning. Jesus you are my hope and faith, trust and love and because of You I do not need human understanding. I have Faith, Hope and Trust in You Jesus and I understand that is all I need!

Yes Jenny's condition changes every day. We have some pretty good days and some rough days. There are some days where I just sit and hold Jenny on my lap. If I let my circumstances determine my mood I would probably cry most of the time. If I did not have Jesus and His word written on the tablet of my heart; I truly would cry in hopelessness every day. I still cry some days but not for Jenny's condition, I cry for people that do not know Jesus or they only know Him and see Him as a bus ticket to heaven. They see Jesus as their liberator, the one that will rapture them out of here. I know where they get that message and I cry some times because they have not experienced the love of Jesus and the hope of Jesus and the trust of Jesus. When Jesus is reduced to a bus ticket to heaven and all you think about is being good enough to get on the bus then you have totally missed the reason Jesus came. Getting out of this world is not the goal!!!! The goal is to transform the world one person at a time like Jesus did! Jesus is our example and we should emulate Him and His work in every way and in every day!!!

For a preacher to teach you to only think of Jesus, as a buss ticket to heaven and limiting faith in Jesus to you having a better day, is truly the biggest tragedy anyone could put on their congregation. I believe that is why I can carry Jenny into so many churches and no one not even the preacher offers to pray for her.

All there hope is in going to heaven not bringing heaven to earth like Jesus did.

The last two Sundays, Jenny and I have been in different churches and both Sundays the preacher has started his service by announcing that half the congregation was out sick. Both of them prayed but neither of them actually commanded the devil to take his hands off their congregation. The devil knows the power we have with faith in the name of Jesus but he has somehow gotten us to just pray for a better day and monetary blessings. That sounds like life is all about me and me having a better day and more money and security in my job. I wonder if Jesus ever worried about having a better job. I remember reading about Jesus feeding about 5000 people with two fish and five loafs of bread. Jesus simply took what he had and blessed it and thanked His Father for it and it was enough for all. Jesus did not worry because he knew he was loved and therefore he knew his Father would provide everything. Sounds like my burden is light and my yoke is easy to me!!! I give you thanks Jesus.

What happened to denying self; you know pick up your cross and follow me!! Jesus is more than our provider, protector, and creator, Jesus is our source of Joy. Jesus said "The Joy of the Lord is our strength. There is no strength in sadness, in fact sadness brings depression and depression makes you want to sleep all the time. We can call it depression, or whatever the doctor calls it but it really is just unbelief. If we just believe in Jesus and His word there would be no such thing as depression.

I see people upset about obama care. I think to myself what do you need it for anyway. If you have Jesus in your heart and not just on your lips the world is at your fingertips. I believe that is why I see so many people unhappy; without the love of Jesus, without His hope and without His Trust. I have no idea what motivates them to get up in the morning. I know spending time with Jesus is and will be my motive forever. I live to be the love of Jesus on the earth. I pray to be Jesus on the earth. Yes Jesus what are we going to do today????

January 10ᵗʰ, 2013

I was holding Jenny on my lap and kissing her when she actually botched her lips up for more kisses. It was in creditable to say the least! I haven't seen Jenny respond like that in over ten years. What a blessing form God! It was so amazing to see her little lips botch up for more kisses. I'm in heaven right here in the camper. Jesus said bring heaven to earth and I experience heaven every day except today it was so real to see heaven in Jenny's little face. Nothing monetary could ever even come close to the Joy of watching Jesus flow through Jenny. I probably give Jenny one thousand kisses a day, but today I received two back and they were right from Jenny's heart. I praise you Jesus for this wonderful time with You and Your daughter Jenny.

January 14th we decided to head to Florida and to warmer temperatures. Jenny and I went to Destin, on the way our brakes on the motor home started locking up really bad. I ask the Lord to send someone really honest and knowledgeable to repair the brakes. Jesus answered my prayer with Bruce's repair service and now the brakes work perfect. Thank you Jesus!!! Thank you Bruce for a great job and a job well done. You know Jesus is so amazing to me! Thinking about the brakes on the camper. They start locking up on the way to Destin, we get to the campground and they have concrete pads to park the camper on. That was a blessing because it made working on the camper a lot easier for Bruce. Then because Bruce comes to the camper to work on our camper, Jenny and I were not inconvenienced in the least. Also the campground we were in had to be willing to let someone work on sight. All that came together and all the parts were readily available. Thinking about all those details coming together is remarkable, and Jesus gets all the praise because He is the one looking out for Jenny and I!!!!

January 17th, 2013

I received a phone call from Joe Coleman my best buddy form the navy. We had talked a couple times since mom died December 21st, but Joe had forgot to tell me about the Christmas card my mom sent him and Renee his wife. In the card mom sent she had hand written these words. "I hope you have a Merry Christmas Joe and Renee, I'm going to be with the Lord this year". Mom had sent the card about 5 days before she died. Isn't Jesus the most awesome God in the world; to have my mom so at piece with death and for Jesus to let me know of her piece through a Christmas card she sent to Joe and Renee? Jenny and I were there the day mom must have written Joe and Renee that card.

January 18th

Jesus gave me the greatest gift. After showering and dressing Jenny I set her on the couch. I had a CD playing a Dan Mohler teaching. As I set Jenny on the couch Dan was saying God loves you, Jenny looked at me and said God loves you as best she could. I could not believe my ears. I just had to think for a minute, I hadn't heard Jenny speak a sentence in years, probably 8 or 9 years at least. I picked Jenny up and put her on my lap and she looked me right in the eyes. I started talking to her, saying Jenny I believe you just said God loves you to me and I believe that came right from your heart. Jesus in His word said from the heart a man speaketh. I believe I just heard from Jesus Holy Spirit, talking right through you, Jenny! Jenny responded by saying yea! I praised God and cried softly for a long time as Jenny fell asleep in my arms. You know I could almost say I live in what some people would call a fiancée world of love. The cool thing is it is not a fiancée it is reality!!!

As I sat there with Jenny I started to realize that Jenny might have something going on with her brain but her heart is still perfect! Jesus in his word tells us to write his word on the tablet of you heart. Jesus said out of your heart a man speaketh. I just heard from Jenny's heart and it was beautiful. Then Jesus confirmed the word with her saying yea. How much more beautiful can life be? I know for a fact that Jesus loves Jenny and I and His love for us goes beyond anything we can comprehend. Thank you Jesus.

On January 21 we went to meet up with Joe and Erin. They invited us to camp with them and some other full time camping families that live on the road. They were all getting together for a rally. We had a great time talking with them and sharing the good news about Gods word. Most of them belong to a campground association called Thousand Trails and said we should join it also and we did. It seems weird to go to a campground and then see ten or so families you already know.

January 29th, 2013

I took Jenny to swim in a heated pool at the campground. I mean Jenny was so relaxed in the water, I hold her in my arms while in the water so her little face is close to mine and we are touching all the time. I know Jenny cannot say that she loves swimming but it is obvious she loves being in the water. I sing to her so softly and Jenny responds as best she can. Today for some reason Jenny had a seizure while in the pool. On our way back to the camper Jenny had another one. We got back to the camper and I had to clean Jenny up, because she was soiled. After I got her on the couch, Jenny seemed to relax some but she was not coming back to base line. I did not panic, I just prayed in total faith that Jenny would be all right, but this time it took an unusual long time for her to come back to base line.

It is amazing to me how I can write and talk about how great God is and how much He loves me but this is where the rubber meets the road and I will see if the teaching from God have traction and is His love really in my heart?

I have talked about or ask the question; in an emergence do you call on God or call on Man (911). The answer for me in this situation is to call on God. Not necessarily because of great faith but because I know the doctors don't have any answers for Jenny's condition. So I just stayed alongside her and prayed, which is the best thing I could do. The problem this time was Jenny was not coming out of the seizer and getting back to base line. As I prayed I kept hearing the words of the doctor saying it will be a big seizer that will take Jenny away.

I ask God how does a doctor have the right to speak these curses over Jenny and then I have to stand in faith and break those words of death off her. I just know to lean not on my own understanding but to draw my strength form the one who made
49

strength. I also know I was hearing form the voice of the devil saying she is dying and I was lessoning. At the same time I was hearing Mathew 7:11 that says;

Mat 7:11 If ye then, being evil, know how to give good gifts unto your children, how much more shall your Father which is in heaven give good things to them that ask him?

In my mind I kept asking God, I know I have ask and I know I have ask in faith and I myself could not do this to a dog or cat so when am I going to see your love manifest in Jenny. I know Jenny is healed but what is taking so long for the healing to manifest in her? Father your word says, how much more shall your Father in heaven give good things to them that ask. I am asking for Jenny's healing to manifest in her now. Jenny condition seemed to be getting worse so I propped her back and head up to help her breath. I finally when to bed with Jenny on the couch, trying to sleep was horrible without Jenny next to me. I kept getting up to check on her.

January 30th, 2013

The next morning I made Jesus and I some coffee. I ask Jesus what was going on with that scripture? Mathew 7:11 seems very clear to me but I could not figure out the timing of it. It seemed as though I was losing faith over it instead of building my faith with it. Jesus asked me, how did the devil tempt me in the desert? I said by misquoting the scriptures when you were very weak from fasting for 40 days. Jesus said you didn't hear that scripture from me yesterday. Here I was upset all day yesterday because I could not figure what Jesus was trying to tell me in Mathew 7:11 and now I find out the voice I was lessoning to was not the Holy Spirit.

Discerning voices can sometimes be difficult. I usually discern by telling if the voice I am hearing is taking me to new heights of Gods love or away from God's love. Yesterday I didn't discern very well because I was dwelling on Jenny's problem. If I had stopped questioning God yesterday and started lessoning to God like I did today I could have walked in the Joy of the Lord and been rejoicing knowing Jenny was just fine and in the hands of the greatest doctor in the world.

Mat 16:19 And I will give unto thee the keys of the kingdom of heaven: and whatsoever thou shalt bind on earth shall be bound in heaven: and whatsoever thou shalt loose on earth shall be loosed in heaven.

I believe the keys of the kingdom of heaven are Joy, Peace and Love of Jesus in your heart and knowing that Jesus is to rock we build our believe on! I separated myself from those believes for couple hours but thank you Jesus for my safe return. I will bind your truth in my heart and in heaven and here on earth my soul shall rejoice with You and I will lose all the earth or fleshly desires to free myself so I am free to do your will here on earth. Jesus you are so special to me and I want to be just like you here on the earth. I pray for your wisdom not to display smartness to others but to pray for others and to have your wisdom and together for us to set others free! I thank you Jesus for setting Jenny and I free of the bondage of the world. My life is your life Father and in You, Jenny and I will live forever.

February 1st, 2013

Today while walking Jenny in the wheelchair I met some people who were so upset about a senate bill that president Obama was trying to pass and they felt helpless to stop the bill, they said Obama is going to ram this down our throats.

As they walked away I was upset because they didn't want to hear anything about God's plan. I thought, I wish they could stop for a moment and think back to what was there biggest concern four years ago, two years ago or even two days ago. If they would think back on the concerns of their past, they would realize they had no power to change them either.

Really all we need to concern ourselves with is being in the will of God. Jesus and the disciples never seemed to be concerned about what the government was doing back then. Their concern was saving souls from the devil's eternal dam nation. They are the example we are to follow. Jesus said my burden is light and my yoke is easy. If we pray to have God change things our government is doing and stand in faith that it will be done, then you can rest that it will be done.

The disciple John tells us "he that doeth the will of God abideth forever" The will of God is so simple, it is to love as Jesus loved, to forgive as Jesus forgave, read your bible to see the example Jesus was for us; don't study it to show how many scriptures you can memorize. Just be Jesus while you are here on the earth. If they had any faith in God they would be praying for President Obama to hear the word of God and let it into his heart, they would pray for Obama to become who God created him to be. We should all pray for obama to hear the word of God and recognize it for the truth it is. It is the truth of God that sets us free from the snares of the devil. Let us pray for Obama and not just complain about Obama.

The best form of worship is to become who we are worshiping, worship Jesus by being Christ like!!!!

Let us be Christ like by emulating Jesus. Jesus never sat around and complained about anything because complaining does not change things. Jesus taught the truth and the truth is we need to pray for our nation. If we spent our time praying and talking to the one who can change things in America, we would have hope instead of hopelessness. We would have faith in our God to change our leaders hearts and God would hear our prayers coming up instead of hearing our complaining that changes nothing.

Jesus warned the apostles about the antichrist in the world. When Jesus spoke this warning He was also warning us. The antichrist are here today and Jesus made it real clear how to recognize them.

> 1Jn 2:19 They went out from us, but they were not of us; for if they had been of us, they would no doubt have continued with us: but they went out, that they might be made manifest that they were not all of us. But ye have an unction from the Holy One, and ye know all things. I have not written unto you because ye know not the truth, but because ye know it, and that no lie is of the truth.

> 1Jn 4:3 And every spirit that confesseth not that Jesus Christ is come in the flesh is not of God: and this is that spirit of antichrist, whereof ye have heard that it should come; and even now already is it in the world.

I don't see how John or anyone can make it any clearer that the antichrist is in the world now and how to determine who the antichrist is. President Obama is an anti-Christ because he "confesseth not that Jesus Christ is come in the flesh." That means that Obama has a spirit of antichrist. Please do not which harm on him but rather pray for him. Our battle is not in the flesh but in the spirit and Obama is just lessoning to the wrong spirit, he is lessoning to the devil, he is manifesting the devil in everything he says and does, we need to pray for him to hear the voice of God. Nothing is going to change if you are not praying for him. Obama is an anti Christ and we all need to pray for his life to be saved, I pray for the love of Jesus to touch his heart and transform it into a life of loving and serving Jesus Christ, amen!!

February 2nd, 2013

2Jn 1:7 For many deceivers are entered into the world, who confess not that Jesus Christ is come in the flesh. This is a deceiver and an antichrist.

Again I have herd people call president Obama an antichrist. He is antichrist because he will not acknowledge Jesus as the Christ Son of the living God! Obama is one of the antichrist! So pray for him to be transformed by the blood and truth of Jesus Christ. Jesus came foreveryone, even the antichrists of the world. We can live in a great country again and we will manifest the love of Jesus Christ to the world. We shouldn't pray to have Obama to be impeached; impeachment would only change the flesh, we should pray for president Obama and his followers to become Christ like. We should pray for America to become Christ like.

February 3rd, 2013

So now we know how to discern who the antichrist are. Jesus also talks about discerning our thoughts. Discerning are thoughts is one of the most important things we will ever learn. The scriptures are very clear that we are to take every thought captive to the obedience of God's word. Let's bring the scriptures into modern day living.

I really do not see how anyone can watch television and discern their thoughts. The actions and words come at you so fast there is no way we can discern our thoughts. If what I am saying about television is not true then why would advertisers pay over a million dollars to advertise for 10 seconds during the game on super bowl Sunday. As we walk through life we have thousands of ten second intervals to demonstrate the love of Jesus and the difference between Christian living and living non-Christian. As Christians we have to make Godly decisions all the time and that can be really hard when we allow ourselves to be distracted by something that is so easily turned off.

I bet there are people reading this right now that will say television is not that bad, I bet they can tell me about commercials on television they saw as a little kid and yet they cannot tell me what the preacher talked about last Sunday at church service. Television has a lasting impact on our lives and it is not always a good impact.

Jesus was so in tune to discerning that He recognized the devil coming through Peter immediately. Peter had traveled with Jesus for three years and still did not discern who he let talk through himself. Remember Peter was not filled with the Holy Spirit yet for Jesus had not died and arouse again.

I found out January 29th   I have a long way to go in discerning my thoughts. I have a great teacher and a best friend to guide me. Thank You Jesus for being my best friend and teacher. The examples Jesus just gave me in the bible are good ones and I will learn from them. Jesus has revealed to me the best way to Hear His Voice is to lesson. Yes lessoning to and for the voice of Jesus is the best way to have relationship with Him. Yes you still have to read your bible to know Jesus because you need His truth to determine what is a lie and what is truth.

Pastor Dan Mohler once said "when you squeeze a Christian you should get a big squirt of Jesus out" those are probably not his exact words but they are close. Dan is saying when you are truly filled with the Holy Spirit and you are put to the test of life; when life doesn't go the way you want it to, don't let the circumstances of life take away your Joy of knowing God. When Jesus was squeezed, love and forgiveness came right out of His heart. We need to be Christ like in every way so I pray that when I am squeezed by life or by someone, I can demon straight the love and forgiveness of Jesus in me. I thank you Jesus for forgiving me for not taking every thought captive and for not recognizing the voice of the devil, while Jenny was having the seizure. When I was squeezed I let some devil in the form of doubt come out but thank You Jesus you were right here to pick me up.

I hope I made that clear, here is another example of being squeezed. I have a friend who was complaining because life was very upsetting. He and his wife were both out of a job for a while. Finally she got a job and a week later he got a good job also. The day he was to start his job, his wife's car had a tire blow out in a bad neighbor. He was still home getting ready to go to his new job when the call came in. He got so upset and was screaming at God; you finally get me a job and now I'm going to be late on my first day. I will probably get fired. He said he went on and on. He finally got her tire changed and on to work. When he explained to his new boss what happened; his boss said settle down, you made the right choice, I would not let my wife stranded in that neighbor either.

The point I am trying to make is we can take matters into our own hands or we can surrender to God. What if the man upon hearing his wife had a flat tire just stopped and prayed for God to send a Christian to change the tire for her. What if he prayed for his boss to understand? He could have been in peace knowing he ask the only one that can; to make good of this situation. Our problem is we just try to solve our own problems in our own strength and then when God makes your boss an understanding boss we don't even know to give the credit to God because we had never ask God in to the situation. If we do see God's hand in our situation, we might even beat ourselves up saying how could I be so stupid not to trust you God!

God is so much more in our life's then we know. We can work our life through God and have peace and rest or we can be in panic mode all the time. When the storm came at sea Jesus was sleeping on the boat. The disciples were going crazy in fear. They woke Jesus up and said don't you care, we are going to drown and you are sleeping. Jesus got up and told the sea to be calm!

> Mar 4:35-37 And the same day, when the even was come, he saith unto them, Let us pass over unto the other side.What was our storm (I have to be at work on time) And when they had sent away the multitude, they took him even as he was in the ship. And there were also with him other little ships. And there arose a great storm of wind, and the waves beat into the ship, so that it was now full.

Our circumstances (the car had a flat tire and our wife is in a bad neighbor) (he screamed at God, you finally get me a good job and now I will be late and I'll probably get fired.) our ship is filling up but we don't acknowledge God is even with us except to complain to him!

> Mar 4:38 And he was in the hinder part of the ship, asleep on a pillow: and they awake him, and say unto him, Master, carest thou not that we perish?

The apostles were in fear just like the man in this story. The apostles even ask God "carest thou not that we perish" it almost sounds funny when they asked Jesus that. It sure isn't funny when we are going through the rough time. The man in our story was screaming at God! Almost like he thought God did not care.

> Mar 4:39 And Jesus arose, and rebuked the wind, and said unto the sea, Peace, be still. And the wind ceased, and there was a great calm.

(and his boss told him calm down you made the right choice.) Right there he should be thanking God and repenting to God for lack of faith.

Mar 4:40 And he said unto them, Why are ye so fearful? how is it that ye have no faith?

(I believe the man when he settled, heard these same words from God) "why are you so fearful? Where is your faith?

Mar 4:41 And they feared exceedingly, and said one to another, What manner of man is this, that even the wind and the sea obey him?

Hopefully we all recognize the voice of God because then we can receive the peace of God. Hopefully we will call on God to calm the storm and change the heart of Obama. I know God will calm the storms in our life if we believe Him and trust Him.

I ask my dear Jesus to bring those scriptures to my mind any time I start to panic about anything. If I have doubt or fear of anything I pray for a remembrance of the disciples in the boat. I also know we have the same power and authority Jesus has and He said we will do bigger miracles then Jesus did. So call on the Name above all names and watch Jesus love us also!

February 4th, 2013

In my coffee time I started thinking about what Jesus said.

Look what Jesus said "why are you so fearful? why is it that ye have no faith?" Jesus will ask us those same Questions someday. I know you could say; but the apostles lived with Jesus and He was right there on the boat with them so why were they so fearful? Actually Jesus is right here with us also. We have His Holy Spirit living in us so why are we so fearful? Why are we without faith? Jesus dwells in us, we can be in continual commutation 24/7. We have better commutation then the apostles did. Jesus is actually living in us! I believe that is the good news that sets us free of worry and unrest. Isn't Jesus the best?

Thank you Jesus for restoring our relationship to even better than it was before Adam ate of the tree of good and evil.

February 8th, 2013

We are still in the same campground and it was 78 degrees in the shade today. I took Jenny to the pool again. She had a great time. I love when I see Jenny so full of joy, it does my heart good and makes taking care of Jenny a real pleasure. I thank you Jesus for these good times with Jenny, these good times bring great Joy to my heart also. Jenny and I are so blessed to be with Jesus 24/7 and that makes life sweet.

While at the pool, a group of older women came to exercise in the water. When they were finished a couple of the women came over to talk to Jenny and I. One woman said this must really feel good to Jenny and I agreed. I mentioned to her that getting Jenny in the pool is really the only time she is off her backside. Another woman asks, "Does she sleep on her stomach?" I said no because her neck is stiff and her head does not turn, if I lay her on her stomach, her face would be planted in the pillow.

I realized I hadn't addressed this in Jenny's book. I hadn't said anything about how immobile Jenny's body is becoming in her first book either. Last night while trying to go to sleep Jenny made a noise and I turned on the light to see if she was all right. She looked like she was trying to smile and I hugged her so tight. Then I started to cry because I realized Jenny's only commutation skills left are noises and some eye expressions where she can make her eyes move.

Her arms move some time but not too much, mostly they just stay crossed across her chest. I really seem to get the best responses out of her in the pool. When I said she was smiling I mean with her eyes not her mouth. I know a couple weeks ago when I kissed her and she bouched her lips for more kisses and it was great for two reasons, one was to see her face mussels move and two Jenny was able to show me, her longing to be loved. I

61

love how she just loves being loved because I love giving her loving. Jenny's sweet loving personality is so beautiful to witness and I just want to thank you Jesus for letting Jenny still share her love with me.

Jesus your love is so strong in my Jenny and I. I know Jenny is not able to communicate like she would if she did not have this condition but you make me know what is going on in Jenny and that is love to the maximum. Thank You Jesus!!!!

February 10th, 2013

While at church the other day a woman came over and while praying for Jenny she put her hand on me and said don't give up hope. She ask God to renew my hope in Him for Jenny's life. I didn't get a chance to talk to her but I knew she was hearing from the Lord because I had been asking God what was changing in my life. I mean I know God loves Jenny and I, and Jenny and I love Him but for the last couple weeks I knew something was missing in my life and I could not figure out what it was.

Thanks to the women in church that spoke out loud the words "don't give up hope" I have my answer from Jesus. Now I know the answer was I was losing hope for Jenny's recovery. I guess I was losing hope for my recovery also. The spider eruptions were on my backside and leg again. They made my bottom hurt to just sit down and the eruptions were on my knee so it was hard to kneel down to put Jenny's shoes on her and my knee was hurting just to walk. There really is no comfortable position when these eruptions act up.

I believe the combination of that and watching Jenny condition declining was becoming over whelming. I believe my hope was fading. This loss of hope was declining so slowly that I didn't see it happening. I knew something was changing but I needed Jesus to help me pin point the problem. I believe the thief that comes to steel, kill and destroy our life is so sneaky that even though I have a great relationship with Jesus I can be deceived by the circumstances of life. I thank God for your messenger and for her hearing form God and then for her to have the courage to speak the truth over Jenny and I.

1Co 13:13 And now abideth faith, hope, charity, these three; but the greatest of these is charity.

You see the top three are Faith Hope and Charity (love). Jesus said without faith it is impossible to please Him and faith is the substance of things hoped for. The last couple weeks I felt like something in me was dying, when the women at church ask the Lord to restore hope in me I knew she was on the right track. I knew Jesus was commutating to me the answer of my prayer through her. Thank You Jesus for the answer to my prayer and THANK YOU JESUS FOR LOVING JENNY AND I SO MUCH!

Jesus answers every prayer concern we have. Sometimes the answer comes through someone that has not herd the question. God you are just so amazing to me and I love You and I love having Hope again. I love seeing another tactic of the enemy destroyed. Hope is one of the top three and so you know without it nothing will turn out right

February 11ᵗʰ, 2013

We arrived at Alliance Coach, a repair center for campers and motor homes. They are going to replace a leveling jack on the motor home. Alliance has their own campground facility so you just stay there until the repair is compete. You can even go out for the day and they will come get your motor home, work on it and put it back on your sight, so you can sleep in it again that night.

February 12th. Lately there seems to be a lot of people who ask me "what do you do all day?" I decided to write down what a day in the life of Jenny and Ron is like.

3:00 AM this morning I was having coffee with my beloved Jesus. We talked for over an hour when I got tired again and went to bed. I woke back up around six thirty and talked to Jesus some more. Jenny woke up at seven, what a blessing Jesus had for me today. Jenny was actually trying to smile at me and her eyes were open wide. I laid alongside her and just hugged her for a while. I am in a little bit of a hurry because we are in a campground where they are going to work on the motor home. One of the leveling jacks is not retracting and the company HWH is replacing it free even though it is out of warranty over three months. This is a big deal to me, you see the jack and labor is around $562.00. Thank you HWH and thank God because carrying Jenny around in the camper that is not level is very hard to do.

I said we are in a bit of hurry because the repair men can come at any time to work on the motor home. I know they would be courteous but I want to be ready.

Jenny's kidneys had let loose, I mean loose, so I put her on the toilet and striped the bed. Her urn soaked through her depends and through both throw away pads and the bath towel I have under her. Today it went into the top sheet and the cover; also

65

into the fitted sheet and mattress pad. I opened the windows to let in fresh air and get rid of the smell.

Before I showered Jenny I set her on the toilet and give her some orange juice. Jenny can drink a whole glass of orange juice before she is showered but some mornings she doesn't seem to remember what the straw is. I have to reminder her by squirting some orange juice in her mouth. It works every day and I Thank You Jesus for her drinking and swallowing. I know your word says nothing is impossible for us that believe and I believe and thank you for your word.

I thank you Jesus for talking to me this morning and every morning, it truly is the most awesome time of the day for me.

I showered Jenny and today is a bowel day so I sported some rubber gloves and cleaned her bowel cavity. It must feel really good to Jenny to get the pressure off. Today she had a lot of gas and seemed somewhat relieved to be done with that. I know I was. I know I Thank Jesus for a lot of things you would take for granted but these are really big blessings from God and I don't want to miss thanking God for them. I like thanking God when I think about it, and thanking Jesus for the easy clean ups.

It is now 8:48am and I'm going to feed Jenny, then off to the laundry. Every day I start Jenny with some greek yogurt. She loves it and so do I. The texture seems to be good for starting her eating. In book one I talked about blending all of Jenny's food but that requirement has gone away again. We can eat out again, especially soft foods like French fries. Lately Jenny has liked cucumbers and melon.

It is 10:09 and I'm off to the laundry which is only a short walk. Two batches today, I usually can get by with one batch if the urn doesn't get into the covers. The blessing here is the machines are big and do a great job. They only cost $1.25 a load to wash and the same to dry. I love the old top loaders that use a lot of water. I mean the water all gets recycled any way and I believe the bigger top loaders do the best job. While I was outside I also took the garbage to the dumpster.

Now I'm going to look up some campgrounds to see where we might go tomorrow, if they get our new Jack on today. It is kind of amazing to watch people in these million dollar motor homes, that is to watch how some of them think they should be the first priority here because they have such important places to be and deadlines to meet. I just feel so blessed by Jesus to not be in a hurry and I'm not sure but I seem to be at more peace then they are. I just pray for them to come to know the Lord Jesus Christ in their busy life and then for them to enjoy what they have. Peace is a precious commodity and is a real gift from God. Nothing else in life can give you peace like knowing God loves you!

10:39 and I am off to put the clothes in the dryer. Upon returning form the laundry I can do what Jenny likes best. I can hold her on my lap and speak life and blessings of walking and talking and the Mind of Jesus into her. I usually hold her until my legs go to sleep. It is so good to see this alertness in her eyes and face. Thank you Jesus for the alertness in Jenny. I love you Jesus.

Jenny and I sat for only a little while when I wanted to go up to the office to see if Will our service rep here at the campground/repair shop could tell me how things were going. After situating Jenny in the wheel chair we went to the office, only to find Will was on his lunch break. Jenny and I went to the laundry and got our clothes out of the dryer. Then back to the camper to change Jenny and fold the laundry and put it away.

12:20pm I got Jenny back into the wheel chair and we went back to the office. Talked to Will and he thought they would get the part on this afternoon. This time while in the office I recognized the receptionist as the one we had talked to last year. We started talking about Jenny and when I told her about the book Jesus and I wrote about Jenny, she wanted one. She complemented me on the cover and said she could not wait to read it. I was excited to see her again because she is going to marry a guy named Ron Johnson. How cool is that?

We stayed in the waiting room for about an hour and a half. It started raining like cats and dogs outside. I had opened the car windows to let the heat out on the way up here. I did not try to run back to close the windows on the car, I just figured it was too late.

In the waiting room, we met a young girl that was born with Williams disease. It seemed to me to be some kind of autism. I prayed for her and she was so cute, she then said her eyes were bad also, so I prayed for her eyes and she added her walking was not that good. It seemed the list could go on and on when her mother said you don't have to tell him everything. But he is praying for me mom she replied, to which I said we will just command everything that is not of God to go in the name of Jesus. Then she took her glasses off and started looking around and said she could see better. Her mom just rolled her eyes and smiled. We talked to her for over an hour with her telling me all kinds of stuff as she held Jenny's hand. I had to get Jenny back to the camper to change her. As we said good by she got up and hugged Jenny for a long hug. She looked at me and said Jenny loves me I can tell and I agreed with her.

When we got back to our camper I checked the car. Remember I said I had opened the windows to let the heat out. While in the office it started raining really hard. When I checked the car there was not a drop of water in the car. Even though I didn't ask God to keep the rain out Jesus kept it out somehow. I truly love you Jesus and the way you look out for Jenny and I. Dry car seats are a big deal and a big blessing for us both. Thank You Jesus for loving us so much as to provide dry seats in the storm.

Around 3:00pm after cleaning Jenny up we ate and then went to look at a campground that is only 10 miles from here. It was a nice ride and Jenny seemed to enjoy it. When we got back to our camper it looked like it might rain again. The woman next to me was having trouble with her gasket on her slide out. I was able to get it water tight with some duct tape, so they could leave their slide out while in the rain and not worry.

I changed Jenny again and then we sat on the couch for a while just holding her on my lap and loving her. I truly love when Jenny is in my arms and she is alert, eyes open and looking at me. Praise you Jesus.

4:30pm and time for coffee. I have some hamburgers thawed to cook on the grill latter but I want to get the sweet potatoes in the oven. Coffee taste great but it is starting to rain again so it might be a pizza night. It is really easy for Jenny to eat pizza and there is one that delivers to this campground. Yes I ask Ron and he said pizza sounds great and he doesn't have to cook. Don't you just love when you can agree with yourself?

4:42pm called the office and they said it will be tomorrow before they can work on our camper.

6:30pm the pizza should be here any time.

6:36pm the pizza is here and Jenny is hungry and so am I. It has been a long time since we had pizza and it really hit the spot. We will have three meals out of this one pizza. Thank you Jesus and for letting it be on sale for $11.00 dollars.

Around 7:00pm and I just got Jenny off the pot, it was a successful trip and another blessing from Jesus. The other day while over at Joe and Erin's camper, Erin was painting the fingernails of their daughter Regan, soon to be five years old. She was so excited to have her nails done. Every finger nail was a different color. When I went to the grocery the next day I bought pink finger nail polish for Jenny, I don't know if she will let me do her finger nails but after watching Regan with hers I'm hoping it will bring a little happiness to Jenny. It could be all in my mind but Jenny seems to like when I cut her hair or shave her legs. I know when we were at Kim and Jim's house last year their daughter Kara did Jenny's nails. Having Jenny's nails done looks a little dome to me but like I said it was so cute watching Regan when Erin did her nails. I thought I would see if Jenny responds like Regan did.

8:30pm and I have been on the phone for a while. Jenny fell asleep on the couch and I did some dishes while talking to Jason on the phone. His hot water heater was not working and we figured out what it was and Jason has hot water again.

9:40pm. It is time to give Jenny her shower and scrub her teeth again.

10:38pm; I just got Jenny in bed and as usual she looks so special at night time. I love having pink sheets and pillow case for her. I love the way Jenny looks at me when I tuck her in. I missed her face and wipe her face a couple times a day but when I do it at night and sing to her Jenny just seems to relax and she realizes it is bed time.

3:01am; I'm having coffee and looking at my notes from yesterday. I finished typing this up and I'm going to have coffee with my best friend and brother Jesus. I'm thinking about the conversation I had with Jason last night and think it is one of the best conversations about God we ever had. Thank you Jesus so much for letting me talk to Jason about my love for You.

4:28am; still typing and lessoning to my brother. For some reason I feel tired like I might go back to bed. Jenny is asleep and I just want to spend some time hugging her. I cannot begin to tell how much I miss Jenny. For some odd reason every time someone touches me, I have an aware ness of how much I mess being touched. The other day in church some people came over to pray for Jenny, some of them were behind us and as they prayed I felt someone's hand on my shoulder. Their hand was warm and it just felt good to be touched, not in any kind of sexy way, not really in a loving physical way just a comforting comfortable way.

I don't know if that makes sense to you but it has been so many years since Jenny and I have talked, or touched. I know someday soon Jenny will wake up out of this condition she is in and we will have real conversation and Jenny will hold my hand as we walk down the path of life again together. That day will not come soon enough for me. I close my eyes and see us walking and talking and touching, I see us holding hands and signing to Jesus about how much we know He loves us. Jesus is real, so real I cannot imagine a day without Him. I can imagine Jenny and I holding hands and talking about all the life still to come.

I remember as a kid being told time and time again "don't get your hopes up to high, you are setting yourself up for disappointment." Now I know the word of Jesus and He says have your hopes sky high for in Him all things are possible. So you might think I am dreaming and not routed in reality but I am routed in the reality of possibilities of Jesus! The word of Jesus is reality to those that believe, so I know just as sure as the sun will come up tomorrow Jenny is healed because the word of Jesus says so. Jesus is my hero and best friend, my brother and the truth that sets us free to be who He created us to be.

5:08am and I'm going to bed to rest in the arms of my best friend Jesus. His word says we can have sweet sleep and I thank you Jesus for it. Amen

7:04 Jenny is awake and alert so lets get started on another adventure. I showered Jenny, the soiled bedding is outside and the windows are open to dissipate the smell.

8:15am and I'm feeding Jenny some yogurt. It is really nice out and cool so I'm going to fix breakfast. We have some baked potatoes to dice up, along with some eggs and presto breakfast is served. Now off to the laundry and today I'm going to disconnect the camper to go over to the dump station to empty the holding tanks.

9:41 am. Will said they are going to try to put the Jack on this afternoon so we can leave tomorrow morning. Good news and thank you Jesus for a great repair at no cost.

10:00 am. Jenny is napping and I'm doing the dishes from breakfast. Then off to the laundry to get our clothes.

11:21 am. Im going to go back to writing Jenny's book. I think this would get pretty boring if I continue to do a play by play. I believe you have a good idea of what life is like minute by minute for Jenny and Ron.

February 14th

We are still at Alliance to have the jack replaced. Our service rep Will told me today they have us on for the afternoon. Around 2:00pm a mechanic came by to install the new jack. Greg started talking to us and instantly I knew he was a Christian and on a wonderful walk with the Lord. His first comment was, "I like your sticker on the back of your camper" COFFEE TIME WITH JESUS. I gave him a track on how that got started.

He seemed really interested in Jenny's condition so I gave Greg the book about her life. Greg got the new jack on our camper in a very short time and had it working perfect, it was truly amazing. He then drove the camper back to our camping sight and ask to pray for Jenny; of course I said yes. His prayer was awesome. He talked about where two or three are gathered in His name Jesus will be there and I believe Jesus lives in us and dwells among us so Jesus was here and is here and lessoning and performing on His word.

Greg also said that we are the church of Jesus and Greg is so right. Jesus is not in a building we call church but Jesus is in us and we are His church wherever we go. I know Greg prayed with sincerity, he prayed with great faith and full expedience! Jenny's healing is a dune deal, Greg's prayer is not going unheard and I will return to Alliance Coach someday with Jenny so he can see the result of his prayer also. I want to thank all the people of Alliance Coach for a great job again and for the great people that work there.

Sunday while attending a church the pastor and his congregation came back to pray for Jenny. One girl put her hand on my shoulder and said I have a word for you from Jesus, Jesus said don't give up hope. I thought to myself this is the second time Jesus told me not to give up hope. I really thought I handled this the first time. I prayed and asked God where I am missing hope. Hope is precious; your word said faith is the substance of things hoped for. Hope is like faith and faith works through love.

Gal 5:6 For in Jesus Christ neither circumcision availeth anything, nor uncircumcision; but faith which worketh by love.

I think my love was faltering which meant my faith was faltering, which means I was not walking in hope. I repented for my loss of hope which ultimately means I was lessoning to the devil and I was letting the signs of Jenny's decline rob me of faith, love and Hope.

If we lose our hope we lose everything this is the second time God has spoken to me about Hope. The fact I am getting the same message from two different people must mean I need to more one on one time with Jesus my source. Jesus and I talked about hope, faith and love for the next couple days and I believe Jesus restored my hope. Thank you Jesus for showing me where I was missing You and lessoning to the devil. I love you Jesus and I always will!!!

You cannot have faith without hope. To me hope is the dream part of faith. I dream of walking with Jenny and holding hands, I dream of having coffee with Jesus and Jenny. Our friend Erin called the other day and said she dreamed we were in a van going somewhere and she ask Jenny a question, Jenny looked up and started talking and answered the question. Erin said I just started crying and held Jenny even closer. In a way you could say faith is the substance of things dreamed for. I know we have all had dreams we hope never come true so I'll stick with the words of Jesus and say Hoped for. I do want to thank you Jesus for the dreams of encouragement! What a delight to even have dreams of Jenny walking and talking and what a delight to have Jesus as your best friend that looks out for you! How do you thank Jesus for blessings like these? I believe you thank Jesus by being like Him!

What is the ultimate way to show you think someone is great? For example; if a young boy likes a certain baseball player, he will want that baseball player's number on his shirt, he will want the same kind of mitt and the young man will watch his favorite player every chance he can so he can emulate the player. I think we call it hero worship.

73

Our worship of Jesus is like that also. I mean we are to emulate Jesus by being like Jesus! We should study the life of Jesus and do as Jesus did and by doing so we are worshiping Jesus. It is so simple to me. Yes I sing in church and I go to church but to me that is not worshipping Jesus. That is fellowshipping with likeminded people and I love it also. You see in my mind I know I am the church and I am to be like Jesus 24/7 not just an hour every Sunday. I want to walk like Jesus, talk like Jesus and most of all I want to love like Jesus. I am blessed to have Jesus as my best friend and Jesus said don't give up hope and I want to honor my best friend with my life. So hopelessness is never going to be part of my life again.

Unlike like the young child emulating the baseball player that doesn't know him; my Jesus does know me and thank you Jesus for even correcting me! Actually My Jesus lives in me and I just let Him love and have His being through me. Thank you Jesus for giving us all a chance to be who you created us to be. I give my life to you Jesus and I thank you for renewing my mind every day. No guilt, no shame, and no condemnation, just love and life more abundantly! Jesus you are the best friend anyone could possibly have.

I remember when Jenny's condition first started; I took Jenny to the doctor and hoped they had some good news that is a good report. When the doctors finally came up with the diagnosis of Picks decease and they told me there is no medicine for it. I started praying for a miracle; at the same time I went to the health food stores and bought all kings of health foods, vitamins, minerals, drinks etc. Jenny and I had taken vitamins for years, while in the Navy I was diagnosed with sugar diabetes. My best friend Joe Coleman's dad told me about vitamins and how helpful they are. I started taking vitamins and shortly after taking them (about a year) I was able to eat everything I wanted again. Jenny and I had a juicier machine; Jenny had read a ton of books on vitamins and health. We even made our own formula for our children when they were babies.

I know there are good effects from taking vitamins. I praised vitamins for getting rid of my diabetes, and praised God for vitamins. I didn't praise God for healing me. Now I just put all

74

my faith where it should have been in the first place, in God. Back then I was Catholic and only though of God for the big things like helping me not sin and keeping me from going to hell. I knew every Sunday at church we said the words "only say the word and I shall be healed" I said it every Sunday but I never saw anyone healed. I don't remember anyone even thinking they would be healed. As a catholic I had faith in doctors and medicine, not God. So I took vitamins and didn't realize it but I put my faith in vitamins, doctors and science not God. When scientist said margarine is better for you then butter, guess what; my mom and every mom I knew fixed everything with margarine.

The very first conference we went to, they said how vitamins and health food could rob you of your faith in God because you were putting your faith in the vitamins. I realized my faith was in vitamins, so I got rid of every vitamin and put my faith, my hope and my trust in God. The funny thing is the very same people that taught me to put my faith in God are now selling vitamins for a living. It is a good thing my belief about faith in God is rooted in scripture and not what others say and believe.

To this very day I have stuck with my decision to put my faith in God. I believe my faith and hope in God is rooted in scripture and in the truth of His Word! I am glad to have made that decision because almost every day I meet someone that says have you tried this or that. I tell them, I believe in God! I believe God!!! If I try everything else along the way, where is my faith and what is it in? I don't want to sound like I am against doctors or science, I just believe they are limited by their own minds and understanding. I believe in God who is unlimited, totally unlimited. I have my faith in God who has no boundaries, who literally can say the word and I am healed!!!!!

Yes I hear the great stories about people that were healed by taking vitamins and I wonder if they are in bondage to vitamins now. That is do they believe without their vitamins they will get sick and die. If they miss a day or go somewhere and forget their vitamins what will happen to them? I believe it is a form of bondage. I know people who have their belief in vitamins and think the vitamins have given them a lot better quality of life here on earth. Like I said I believed that for years.

I hear people say it's the flu season again and every year they get the flue shot and every year they still get the flue. Someone once said the definition of insanity is to do the same thing over and over expecting a different outcome. If you expect bad things like the flue to come your way the devil will oblige you with the things you are giving him permission to give you. My faith is in God and I haven't had the flue in ten years or more! I am not insane because I expect a good out come and I get it. Thank you Jesus for the truth that sets us free and gives us rest in you.

Suppose I started giving Jenny vitamins and supplements etc and Jenny was suddenly healed, where should I put or to whom shall I give the praise to. I have heard of people with cancer talk about a doctor in New York, who said to do this and to eat that" and when they followed his advice they were healed of cancer. Then they praised him for their healing, not God and I wonder what God thinks? What if the doctor in New York told everyone to drink ten glasses of carrot juice every day and make sure the carrots are organic? The world would run out of organic carrots in no time at all and then what would we do? Maybe pray for God to send more organic carrots?

Are we to live in our own strength or let the joy of the Lord be our strength? I will not change my faith in God and that is where I will be the rest of my life. I know when I stand before Jesus for judgment I can say all my faith is in you Jesus and you alone. I do pray for Jesus to bless the decisions I make and I know He does when my decisions line up with His teachings. Jesus turned water into fine wine instantly, He did miracle after miracle instantly. My faith, my Hope, my Love and my TRUST are in Jesus the creator of us all, not in organic carrots. Why would anyone put their faith in scientists and their findings when you can put your faith in the one who created us all and knows all?

Jesus in his word talked about rest.

Mat 11:28-30 Come unto me, all ye that labor and are heavy laden, and I will give you rest. Take my yoke upon you, and learn of me; for I am meek and lowly in heart: and ye shall find rest unto your souls. For my yoke is easy, and my burden is light.

Are we resting in God if we have to take four glasses of carrot juice every day? Are we resting in God if we have to read every ingredient in everything we eat? Jesus said not to worry so are we going against His commandment when we worry about what we eat. Just ask Jesus to bless everything you put in your mouth and ask Jesus to help you make healthy decisions. Jesus really wants to be that personal with you. So let Him! Jesus turned the water into fine wine and He will do the same thing for us. Ask Jesus to bless your food and He will bless it with what you need.

Diligently seek Jesus with all your heart.

Heb 11:6 But without faith it is impossible to please him: for he that cometh to God must believe that he is, and that he is a rewarder of them that diligently seek him.

When we stand before Jesus for judgment I believe Jesus will be more concerned about how much we trusted Him than anything else. I see trust in the bible to be all inclusive, that is Faith Hope and Charity all in one word. In Hebrews 11:6 you see without faith it is impossible to please Jesus. God said we must believe Him, that is not a suggestion, it is a commandment! Jesus is a rewarder of them that diligently seek Him. You diligently seek Jesus by getting the world out of the way. I mean when we put the things of the world in front of Jesus "like I did for 50 some years" yes for 50 some years I thought I needed to work to provide for Jenny and our children. I only talked to Jesus when I needed Him and only about what I needed from Him. I never talked to Him about why I was here and if Jesus needed me to do anything for Him. Thank You Jesus that has all changed!

To diligently seek anything you must set your mind on achieving the thing you seek. No one can learn anything without wanting to learn it. You must have the desire to know God, if you are going to become friends with Him. When you fell in love with your wife you were diligently seeking to know her, to please her and give of yourself to make her happy. A relationship with Jesus is the same way; He wants us to fall in love with Him, to seek Him, to desire to please Him and to desire to spend time to know Him intimately. Jesus will be your best friend if you let Him. Please let Jesus be your best friend, I did and I will never regret it!

February 18th, 2013

We went to Spring Hill Florida to see Tony and Cal our neighbors from Pond Run Rd. It was nice to see them and catch up on how they are doing. They also paid for half our camping fee, which helped us a lot. Jenny and I went to a church service that was close to our campground on Sunday morning. We were a couple minutes late so I had to park close to the church door, and because I was late I chose to carry Jenny into the church rather then put her in the wheel chair. One of the ushers moved our car for us, when he came back in he handed me my car keys and said don't leave until you talk to me after church.

The service was really nice and the people were friendly, we even got to talk to the preacher for a couple minutes. Then Tyrone the man that parked our car for us came over and said all through the service he kept hearing God tell him to give us a newer car. I was elated, surprised and overcome at the same time. Tyrone had never met us before; he told me he owns a car lot in Tampa. I ask how he could just give away a car and he said the cars were never mine in the first place. They belong to my Father in heaven and He says to give you one. When we left the church I was in heaven because a couple days before that I had tried the air-conditioning in our car and it did not work.

On Monday we went back to thousand trails campground again, after being there a couple days we met Scott and his wife Janet and their family of five. Scott's voice was soft and had a calming effect on Jenny and anyone he talked to. We hung out with his family for a couple nights and they were awesome. Scott has a great relationship with God that transcends down to his wife and children.

His children had the prettiest eyes I had ever seen. One night while walking Jenny in the wheel chair, I saw Scot walking and we stopped to talk, when Jenny heard his voice she turned her head and looked up at him, then she gave him the biggest smile. Scott was excited to see her reaction and I just came out of my own skin to see Jenny smile that big. For months now Jenny would try to smile but her face mussels did not cooperate. This was truly a blessing from God to see Jenny's beautiful smile again! Thank you Jesus for this special night.

While at the campground we met another couple and became friends. Mary and Reed Alison. What a friend ship this is turning into. They invited Jenny and I to Brookside church where they were going on Sunday morning. We went and Mary and Reed were right. The church is great and the worshiping of Jesus was super. It is a satellite church of the Andrew Womack churches and schools. From Pastor Wade, to the entire congregation the people were on fire for the Lord and the Truth of the gospel message. It is always a blessing to be part of a worship service but here the worshiping was so real and right from the heart. Jesus said from the heart a man speaks and when a congregation speaks from their heart in union with God; look out big things are going to happen.

The church has a school on Monday and Thursday night. Jenny and I went with Reed and Mary, I love going and hearing the word taught correctly, but the best part was the time Reed, Mary, Jenny and I spent talking about God. The only thing better then fellowshipping with like minded people is actually doing the word of God and seeing miracles.

March 2013

After observing Jenny and I a fellow camper ask how do you do doctors while traveling full time? I said I only have one doctor and He makes camper calls. She looked at me like I'm nuts. Then I said Jenny is healed and she knew I was nuts.

I guess I need to talk about Jenny's condition for a few minutes so you will know what is going on in our life that is what the fellow camper was seeing in the physical. Jenny's physical condition seems to be getting worse. I am not pronouncing that on her, I am just trying to convey what is going on physically. Smiling takes a lot of effort for Jenny; her face mussels do not cooperate with her desire to smile. Swallowing is a big effort also for Jenny; it seems to be a really big discussion. Jenny falls asleep even while chewing her food.

Most of the time it is very hard to tell if Jenny can see. She will have her eyes open and looking at me but when I touch her she jumps. I used to be able to get her to drink from a straw. Now she doesn't seem to recognize what it is in her mouth. Feeding her can take an hour and a half. For a while Jenny seemed to like eating out where there was a lot going on to stimulate her. Now that doesn't seem to make a difference. Foods that used to bring a smile on her face and a little excitement in her life, just doesn't work anymore. I guess the worst part is how Jenny seems to get so frustrated and the blood vans in her face and arms look like they are going to pop out of her skin. It is really ugly to see.

Jenny's body is starting to bend like the letter C. When I hold her on my lap she is bent in a C and now her body is staying in the C shape. Her arms are crossed on her chest. Her hands are fisted all the time and her legs are crossed all the time. Showering her is a little difficult in the position she is in. I can see why people who don't know God and only look at the physical would think I am nuts for saying Jenny is healed. Please read on and you will see I am not nuts! Jenny is healed; I have the word of Jesus Himself to believe in.

Traveling has become more difficult. I mean it is more difficult for me not Jenny. It is more difficult for me because I miss her so much. When Jenny is awake she seems to get fidgety and the only way to settle her down is to hold her on my lap and talk to her. When Jenny is setting on my lap, she looks at me as I talk to her and she relaxes to where she falls asleep. I usually hold her until my legs go to sleep and start to hurt. As soon as I move her she wakes up and starts getting fidgety again.

You might be thinking that I am spoiling her and I am, but I love it when I can just stop what I am doing and hold her on my lap. She relaxes in my arms to the point where she is like a wet washrag. I can move her arms and open her little fist, I can uncross her legs and I believe these are good things. I know it is difficult to dress her with her legs crossed and her arms crossed on her chest. When I do travel I do not set goals I just go as far as I can and let that be good enough.

Now for the good news about Jenny! Jenny and I are blessed to have a relationship with Jesus and Father God and through the Holy Spirit have the same life giving power, the healing power, the salvation power and power over the devil and his works. I have the same power and authority as Jesus gave the apostles, thank you Jesus.

Sometimes I wonder what people who don't know Jesus as their savior do in times like these. Jesus says to walk by faith and not by sight. Jesus is life and life more abundantly. Jesus called the apostles, trained them and then sent them out to teach the kingdom of God has come upon you, Jesus also sent the apostles out to train others to heal the sick, raise the dead and cast out demons. The apostles preached the kingdom of God and then they passed their relationship to God on to the church. We are His church; we are Gods chosen people if we chose to be. We are ambassadors for Jesus! I'm a son of the living God and because I know God loves me, I can look at Jenny and know she is healed! If you think I am a nut or crazy for saying Jenny is healed, go ahead think I'm a nut, that is okay; God calls me his SON!!!

I would rather be walking with faith in my Jesus and be thought of as nuts than to be smart in your eyes! You say, I need to look at reality; Jenny is getting worse, you say don't get your hopes up to high Ron you will only be disappointed. Why would I believe you or men that tell me "protect your heart Ron; don't be a fool Jenny is dying right in front of you." People think I am living in denial; people say I'm living in some kind of finesse world because I believe in God. In God there is no such thing as having your hopes to High! "All things are possible" In God there is no disappointment! "All of God's promises are true" The people that say I am crazy or a nut case need to know God is real, God is truth, God loves me and those people need to experience the love of God! I'm not nuts, I'm just peculiar and I love it!

> Deu 14:2 For thou art an holy people unto the LORD thy God, and the LORD hath chosen thee to be a peculiar people unto himself, above all the nations that are upon the earth.

Yes I am a peculiar person to you but I am beautiful to my Father in heaven and He has chosen me to take unto himself. If I am nuts I want to stay that way for eternity.

The people that say I'm nuts, need to have a relationship with Jesus. I remember when I went to mass every Sunday and Holiday and received Jesus into my heart through communion. It was so wonderful to know Jesus was in me until the host dissolved. I could talk to Him for a few seconds. Yes I had the body and blood of Jesus Christ in me for a few seconds.

When you really start to seek a relationship with Jesus and you put Him first in your life, you will come to the truth that Jesus wants to be in us and with us, to talk to us and His plan is for us is to manifest Jesus 24/7. Communion was not just at the last supper and every time you rein act the last supper. Communion is for every second of your life! Along with that revelation I realized Jesus loves me and the two of us can talk, laugh, walk and cry together. In fact we live together as one, I am one with Jesus and I know the life giving power of Jesus flows through me as it did the life giving power of God the Father flowed through Jesus the man while He was on the earth.

I want to put to rest the words I used in the last paragraph (rein act the last supper) rein act is a poor choice of words, it sounds like we are acting; Jesus said

Luk 22:19 And he took bread, and gave thanks, and brake it, and gave unto them, saying, This is my body which is given for you: this do in remembrance of me.

THIS DO IN REMEMBRANCE OF ME! Jesus said this is my body and blood as he took bread and wine and blessed it in to His body and blood. I think people have been arguing ever since weather or not this is symbolism or did Jesus really change bread and wine in to the body and blood of Jesus?

To me the answer is so simple because Jesus came to show us life is really in your spirit. In the beginning Jesus breathed Spirit life into dust to make mankind in his image.

Gen 2:7 And the LORD God formed man of the dust of the ground, and breathed into his nostrils the breath of life; and man became a living soul.

Isn't that cool, Jesus breathed life into the dust. I believe it because God said it! I don't need any other proof. Life is in your spirit. Jesus loves us all, He proves His love by dying for us all. I believe it! Do you?

I believe the whole bible is true and I cannot figure out why is it so hard for some people who claim to be believers to believe Jesus changed bread and wine into the body and blood of Himself? Again Jesus said it, so I believe it. For me it is easy to say Jenny is healed because Jesus said so in His word. If you cut your finger, you expect it to heal. It is easy to believe the little cut will heal because you have seen it so many times. I ask you who made the blood that has to flow through your body to sustain life and then suddenly become a clogging agent when you cut yourself. If you said only a genius could make such a thing your right. God is my God, and God is my genius, God is my healer and God is best friend. You can say I'm crazy but God says I'm His Son!

I just believe what Jesus said in His word, there is really no arguing the point in my mind, Jesus said He created the world and I believe it! What is there to argue about? Jesus came and changed keeping the law from physical to spiritual. Jesus said to renew your mind, to be baptized into the Spirit, to live in the spirit and your battles are spiritual, Jesus said without faith it is impossible to please Him. Faith is your heart belief or better put it is your spiritual belief.

I can tell you this by FAITH I receive Jesus in to my heart 24/7 and by FAITH I live with Jesus in me renewing my mind to live the word of God made flesh by turning my fleshly desires into Spiritual desires of being like Jesus. THANK YOU JESUS!!!!!

I also believe in God all things are possible so why would I not believe Jesus when He said THIS IS my body and my blood, to me that settles it, there should be no argument! It is His body and blood. Jesus did not say this symbolizes my body and blood. Jesus said THIS IS!!!!!

Mat 26:26-28 And as they were eating, Jesus took bread, and blessed it, and brake it, and gave it to the disciples, and said, Take, eat; this is my body. And he took the cup, and gave thanks, and gave it to them, saying, Drink ye all of it; For this is my blood of the new testament, which is shed for many for the remission of sins.

I have the word of God to believe in! The words THIS IS are so simple for me to believe, what I don't understand is where all the unbelief comes from. Jesus is in my heart 24/7, we will live together forever! When people tell me I need to protect my heart I tell them Jesus is my protector. You see my heart is protected by the love of Jesus! Jesus said to bring heaven to earth, to do that, ask Jesus into your heart and start living in heaven now, heaven is not the destination, heaven is Jesus living in you NOW!!!!

Doctors study for years and years to become a doctor and then they have to read updated material all their life to stay up with the changes in medicine. My doctor wrote one book and it has stood the test of time for thousands of years, with no updates. I believe my doctor and when I go to my doctor I don't have waiting lines to see Him, I don't have deductibles, I don't have insurance contracts, I have FAITH, I have TRUST, and that gives me HOPE and most of all I have God's word for life more abundantly.

If you lesson to people talking about doctors long enough you will hear stories about doctor's mistakes and doctors not caring! I'm tired of hearing about side effects of man-made medicine! I'm tired of hearing these words "sometimes you have to get worse before you get better or what alternative do you have?" Where is that in the bible? I don't watch television but I hear people talk about all the new diseases that are being promoted on television. I really don't understand how people can think I'm the one that is nuts.

I don't have any of their diseases and I thank God for His word that says disease is captivity from the devil, the devil said he came to steel, kill and destroy our life. I cannot think of a better way to describe sickness then killing, steeling and destroying your life. You don't have to be sick too long to realize the truth, your sickness is (steeling) your life, sickness can (kill) you and sickness is (destroying) your life. Jesus was very clear about who came to kill steel and destroy you. Jesus said I am life and the truth that sets us free!!! THANK YOU JESUS FOR TRUTH, LIFE AND LOVE!!!!!

How can people put their faith in doctors that advertise on television? For example, Doctors advertise, "If you have these signs, you have restless leg syndrome" and we have a pill for you. The day before they started advertising almost no one had even heard of restless leg syndrome. Then they tell you the side effects of the medicine will probably kill you but your legs won't hurt and we will be rich so come see us now. Now that is a side effect your doctors can live with. It is really hard to understand how people can say "I'm the one that is nuts."

I don't want to put all your doctors down because there are some really good ones out there. True fully I might not be here if not for doctors. Before my faith was this strong for God; doctors were all I had to keep me alive and I thank God for them.

Now I thank God for faith; through God's truth my faith in Jesus has grown over the years to let me be so in love with Jesus and trust in Jesus that I put my life in His hands. If your faith in God is not that strong then by all means go to the doctor so you can live to have another day to seek Jesus and trust in Jesus. Jesus will meet you where your faith is!! Actually that is another way God shows He loves us; God is extremely patient and will work through doctors if we ask him too until our faith grows to be in Him alone. Thank you Jesus for truth and faith and grace and

85

letting us live until we understand your love for us enough to TRUST IN YOU ALONE!!!!

Is a person a nut if they love and trust Jesus? I live to hear from Jesus. I live to be with Jesus and walk with Jesus, and talk to Jesus. I live to be like Jesus, that is to preach His word boldly, to heal the sick, to raise the dead and to cast out devils. To set the captives free is my desire and with Jesus living in me; nothing is impossible for me. Trusting in God is like breathing to me, knowing God is all powerful is wonderful to me, but knowing the creator of the universe loves me, is life and life more abundantly to me. He knows me personally, He hears me, and Jesus is so real I can talk to Him like you talk to your doctors, the difference is with Jesus there are no evil side effects! The best knowledge you can gain in life is, God wants to call you His son; yes God wants you to be so close to Him that He knows you by name!

With Jesus I get love! Real love, not sympathy that creates a desire for more sympathy. I do not have bills that add to the tress and I don't live in captivity of medicine and doctor appointments. I live in freedom of asking God what are WE going to do today? I love my Jesus and His freedom from all sickness; Jesus is freedom form disease and freedom from death! I'm not nuts; the way you think of nuts but I am free and I don't live in fear or in need of sanitizer to keep germs away. I'm in love with Jesus and the side effect for loving Jesus is everlasting life! I believe in Jesus and the side effect of believing Jesus is Joy, Peace, Faith, Hope, freedom from fear, perfect health and knowing the perfect love of Jesus is for us 24/7!!!! Don't forget you can be a Son of God too!

I see people healed instantly; when they hear the word of God preached! I see the lame walk; I see the Joy in the hearts of people that hear the word of hope from Jesus and that is what Jesus came to do, give us Hope! Trusting in Jesus is SETING THE CAPTAVIES FREE. Forgiveness is freedom, health is freedom, a life of Joy is freedom and life starts with an intimate relationship with Jesus. I simply put my trust in God and his words of truth! The word of God has not changed for thousands of years and I believe God is the final word! I know God's love is all I Need and I know God loves me so I am being purified daily. Ask God for truth and Seek God for relationship and I guarantee Jesus will hear your prayer and answer your prayer with truth that sets you free!

Joh 8:32 And ye shall know the truth, and the truth shall make you free.

The truth in the bible is setting Jenny and I free from all sickness and all infirmities! Jesus is purifying us, watching over us and most of all JESUS IS LOVING US. I no longer pray for the sick and down trotted because nowhere in the bible did Jesus say I will pray for you. Jesus just commanded sickness to go, Jesus is our example; I follow Jesus and I just command the sickness to go and it has to go! If your faith is not their then go to the elders and their prayer of faith will save the sick. Notice it is the prayer of faith, not the prayer of fear! THANK YOU JESUS for making your love so clear! Yes thank you Jesus for making Jenny and I peculiar!!! We are so blessed to know your love for us!! I could write a book a thousand pages long and still not thank God for everything He has done. I love being peculiar!!!

Jesus and Jenny and I love you and we pray for you to be peculiar too! Are you a Son of God? Does God know your name? Is your name written in the book of life? The answers to these questions can all be YES if you just ask God for intimacy with Him and trust Him for a real relationship. Speaking about is your name written in heaven's book of life; I believe all our names our written in the book of life. Jesus called it the book of life so if we have life, all our names are in it. The question should be "is your name crossed out of the book of life?" Yes we have the power to remove our name from the book of life by the choices WE make!!! Choose well eternity can be heaven or hell.

It is my desire for everyone to know God so well that you will proclaim His word boldly and bask in the perfect love of God that frees us from all fear and sends the devil packing back to Hell! Life is easy when you trust God!!!

March 25th, 2013

I decided to move on today. We were going to go to Kentucky for family week but I changed my mind. Reggie offered to pay for our camping while there, which was so nice of him and Joyce. Jenny and I were looking forward to going and seeing everyone so the decision not to go was a hard one. I talked with one of the Waller boy's and they said the campground was full and they had like 40 extra families signed up. The last two years when we went up that way we also went to see our sons in Cincinnati. This year would be different because we haven't been to Carrabelle Beach yet. So I would have to drive 865 miles to Kentucky and then drive 600 miles back to Carrabelle Beach. It seemed like a lot of miles for one week. I must say I am already regretting not going. I am missing out on all the fun, all the fellowship, but most of all I'm missing the love that flows so freely there. I new I would miss not going and I do! I think I should have gone because I miss the fellowship there and I miss the love there!

At my mom's funeral, back in December I saw my cousin Chuck Johnson and found out he now lives in Florida. He told me to call him when we go to Florida so we could visit. It turns out his house was right on our way to Carrabelle Beach so we found a campground nearby and visited for a couple days. It was really cool to hear about his life and what his children are doing. Jenny and I are so blessed to be able to go where ever we want and Jesus simply puts people in our path that make traveling so much fun. We had a great time visiting with Chuck and Pat his wife. They are both blessed with great health and blessed with a close relationship with their children. Jenny and I were blessed to be with them and look forward to seeing them again real soon. I want to thank them for such a great time and thank God for putting us together.

Thank You Father God and Jesus for this special visit with Chuck and Pat!

March 28th, 2013

Jenny and I are heading toward Carrabelle Beach but we are stopping at a place called Lake City Florida for a couple days. Curtis and his family are going to stop by Friday. I am excited to see them and hopefully hear the girls sign. I'm looking so forward to it. I can't wait to see Noah's little face and hear him say God bless you Ron. They are great examples of what a God centered family looks like and lives like. Jenny and I love to be around them, we love see their love of God shine; I know why God said we are the light of the world. When you're around someone that glows the love of Jesus you cannot help but want to glow a little brighter also. Jenny and I are looking forward to Friday and the loving family we will spend time with. Most mornings I get up and ask the Lord what are WE going to do today. On Friday I already know God has something great planed and I thank Him for our visit.

Our visit did not go as well as planned. Jenny and I camped at a campground called Oaks and Pines camping resort. When Curtis arrived with his wife and children, I ran over to meet them when suddenly the owner started telling Curtis to park his van straighter in the huge grass parking area. At first I thought the owner was kidding because the request he made; made absolutely no since at all. Then I realized he was serious. We were the only ones there and it was raining, no one else was coming, it just did not seem like a big deal. So Curtis said yes I will move my van and ask if he could just get his children out and under the pavilion first. The owner said get you kids in that van and get off my property. When I tried to reason with him I got kicked out also. Four years on the road and my first kick out. Wow! After I unhooked our camper I went to the office to say good by, I told them I didn't know what happened out there but I will pray for them.

I really feel sorry for that guy because I used to have an explosive temper like his. I am so blessed to know Jesus and have Jesus in my life now. So I sent the owner of the camp ground a copy of the teaching I have from the Lord called Mad. I hope it gives him some insight to what triggers a temper, I know it has sure helped me. I will continue to pray for him so he can open his heart to the Lord! Really I am blessed to know him because I saw firsthand how far the Lord has brought me out of the bondage of self-hatred. I truly love you Jesus and thank You Jesus for loving me!!!! Thank You Jesus for freeing Me!!!

Curtis and family; Jenny and I went to a rest area on interstate 10, we grilled out in the rain and ate in our motor home. We really had a better time than we would have had under the pavilion because the motor home was warm and dry. After they left to go back home I decided to stay in the rest area for the night.

The next couple days we stayed at another campground because Carrabelle Beach RV resort was still full.

Wow we are finally going to Carrabelle Beach RV resort.

On the way to Carrabelle I started writing a little teaching to read to pastor Dons congregation. Here it is!

SICKNESS AND FAITH

First I want to thank Pastor Don for being such a good friend and a very good Pastor! Coming back to Carrabelle and the good people of his congregation is like coming home to a good home for Jenny and I. The warm hearts of everyone here has given us light and warmth. It is true the special people of Don's congregation are good people and a true blessing to be around.

You might wonder why I used the word good to describe Pastor Don and all of you. I could have very easily used the word great or greatest or excellent or superior to describe all of you. I chose the word good because when Jesus spoke the world into existence He said "it is good" and when Jesus was finished He called His creation "very good". In my pursuit to be like Jesus I am trying to use His words in my vocabulary. Plus I think when we try to describe people in better terms then good it is like putting down good and maybe elevating us to a higher standard. I remember in

Mar 10:18 And Jesus said unto him, Why callest thou me good? there is none good but one, that is, God.

So calling you good is putting you in some very good company! Most of the people here know Jenny and I have been coming to Carrabelle Beach for four years now. Probably everyone here has lost a loved one. Most people would say losing a loved one is never easy. I lost my mom December 21/ 2012; she was 93 years old and really she was ready to go. In my heart I felt as though Jesus sent her an angle and ask her if she wanted to spend Christmas on earth or in heaven. Mom chose heaven. I can tell you this 5 days before mom died, Jenny and I were setting with her having coffee, mom talked and walked to the bathroom. She was alert and her only complaint was, she said her body hurt. Two days later I received a phone call from my sister saying mom had taken a turn for the worse. Mom died two days later in her own bed with her loved ones being around her and we were all in peace knowing it was the right timing of the Lord Jesus Christ calling her home. I don't feel as though I lost my mom I feel like she decided to go home to her final reward.

I believe that is how death should be. I can tell from watching people's reactions that most people for the last eight or nine months have looked at Jenny like she should be in a home or better yet I should release her spirit to go be with the Lord. I believe sickness is from the devil. The devil's mission is to kill, steel and destroy our lives. One look at Jenny and most people would say the devil is succeeding in his mission.

If you go by the outward signs, or the circumstances you would be right. I guess that is why Jesus told us not to look with our eyes or think cardinally minded. As soon as you look at the problem, you will take your mind off Jesus and the fact you have His Holy Spirit living in you and you will start feeling weak and helpless to solve the problem. You run to the doctor who only has the knowledge to practice medicine. You are falling right into the hands of the devil.

Jesus said it is the prayer of faith that will heal the sick, not the prayer of fear. We are to have the mind of Christ and eyes of Christ and the love of Christ in us and flowing through us. We are to be like Jesus looking down on our problems not like helpless humans looking up through our problems. From God's vantage point, which is our vantage point when we have the eyes of Jesus, even mountains seem small. We are to speak to the problem and command it to change, don't talk to God about the problem; He already gave us the answer. Jesus gave us the same power over the devil that He has. Just believe and use your power!

A lot of people who pray for someone will talk to God about the person they are praying for. Almost as though God does not know the sick person. They talk to God about the problem or when we talk to God about our self's, we talk to God about our problem. Don't pray the problem, it takes no faith to pray the problem or to ask God for help, but Jesus said it takes a prayer of faith to save the sick. A prayer of faith is praying the answer God gave us for the problems. Jesus showed us compassion by

93

commanding devils to leave, Jesus commanded sickness to leave, Jesus forgave us all our sins and Jesus showed compassion by raising the dead for us the living.

Jesus did all these things by having relationship to His Father, a loving spiritual relationship! Jesus said our battle is spiritual and our armor is spiritual! We accept the fight physically and we do an exceptional job physically and physically we are very compassionate. Jesus commands us to be compassionate physically, so taking care of the physical needs of others is very God like and is very pleasing to God. God just wants us to be that compassionate in the spiritual battle also. Jesus wants us to have relationship with Him so when the battle comes we are ready spiritually and physically to do His will on earth. Jesus would never command us to do something; without giving us the tools to do it with. So we have the command and the tools, let us put them to use and have some fun. Just believe in God's word!

Jesus said when He comes back we should have the devil under our feet. Jesus gave us the same Holy Spirit that raised Him from the dead. I have the Holy Spirit of Father God and Jesus living in me! There is nothing that can get in His way except my unbelief. Fear is of the devil and fear is faith in the devil, fear is unbelief and fear will rob you of faith. Don't give way to it. Just believe in God!

We are to know the will of the Father and to do His will! To know His will look to the words of Jesus who said He came to reveal the Father to us. Jesus was perfect love so the Father is perfect love and we can be perfect love if we are surrendered to the Father and have relationship 24/7. Jesus is perfect love; Jesus is the perfect love that cast out fear (devil). Look to the bible and read how Jesus took charge over every situation. Don't read the bible and try to figure out if this is true, just believe the one who said "He cannot lie" and accept the bible as truth. Accepting the bible as true is the childlike faith Jesus talks about. The more you believe the more you are set free. Jesus said my truth will set you free. I know the more of the truth of Jesus you have in your heart the harder it will be for the devil to talk you into sinning. Just believe in the word of Jesus and you are set free of the devil and you are free of his sinning nature! We do not have a sinning nature; we are made in the image of God; so we have to except a sinning nature from the devil to have one. Just cast it off.

Jesus was a man while on the earth and was as human as we are. Yet I never read anything about fear being in Him. He is our example to follow and look up to. Let the love of Jesus in your heart and watch fear flee. Just believe and let Jesus in your heart and be free.

Circumstances do not dictate the outcome of sickness, YOU DO!!! With Jesus and Father God dwelling in you, you BETTER dictate the outcome. Jesus did not die just to be the atonement for sin! Jesus came to show us we have power over DEATH and so death does not exist, we just leave here for judgment, and we should only leave when Jesus calls us home, not from sickness that we have God's power over. Jesus describes sickness as captivity and bondage, which is how we should describe sickness. Sickness is not picks disease; sickness is not cancer or any other name we give it! Sickness is captivity and bondage. Jesus said He came to set the captives free and He did and so can we!!!! Just believe!!

Jesus also told us to take every thought captive to the obedience of His word. If you're watching television, I can guarantee; you are not taking every thought captive and I can guarantee you; the Lord that sent His only Son to teach us and be our example in life, will not talk over the noise of the television. Be sill and hear His voice. You want the truth that sets you free just be still and Hear His Voice! Get up in the morning and ask yourself what does Jesus want to do today? For some reason we think life in God is all about God helping us have a nice day. Again that is the reverse of what our life should be. We are here to do the work of the kingdom! Ask the Lord every morning "what are we going to do today." Ask Jesus who do you want set free today and He will lead you to someone that He wants set free! Watching someone set free is Joy beyond our understanding!!! I want that every day!!!

Kingdom work is lessoning for our marching orders and then doing them. Jesus said over and over I only do what I seen My Father do. What did Jesus do? He healed, forgave, cast out devils (set people free) raised people from the dead and preached the word boldly. So we can say I only do what I have seen my Father

95

do! Jesus gave you and I the same set of orders and by faith we can complete them. Just believe! Jesus would not ask you to do anything, without giving you the power to do it. Jesus said you were given the measure of faith so what is holding you back?? Maybe you don't believe Him. That would be a tragedy. Jesus died for me and I will not waste my time trying not to sin when I can spend my time glorifying God by believing Jesus lives in me. That is taking the tragedy of nonbelief and turning it into the MAGESTY OF BELIEF!! I'm set free and I thank you Jesus!!!!

Don't wait for someone else to do it, you will be missing out on all the fun! You will miss the Joy and the love of Jesus. You only have one life to give so make the best of it for Jesus. You are the best Jesus has and Jesus is okay with that. The devil is the one that makes you feel insignificant!!! I hear Christians say "oh Lord bring the rapture, I want out of here" I think to myself that sounds REALLY self-centered. Not all my loved ones are saved so I know I need more time. I pray for God to put off the rapture! Please don't think for one second you don't have a mission to accomplish because you do! Please don't say I can't because with Jesus in you failure doesn't exist. Just believe and nothing will hold you back!

Don't read the bible to see if it is true, don't argue with it!!! JUST BELIEVE IT!!!! CHILDLIKE FAITH IS NOT AN OPTION!!! Childlike faith is praise worthy! Power and authority are yours for just believing!!! If you need proof or have an argument in your mind about anything you read in the bible you are in doubt and lessoning to the devil! Just believe what you read in God's word. When I read the bible I put myself in the place of Jesus. If the bible says Jesus raised Lazarus from the dead then I read Ron raised Lazarus from the dead. It is simple Jesus said for us to raise people from the dead and so we can. Just believe.

If I look at the circumstances of my life; I see the deter ration of Jenny's condition. The circumstances will make me think death is coming real soon. The circumstances make me look like I'm crazy for saying I believe the word of God. Am I crazy to declare Jenny is not going to die of this disease? Am I crazy to declare Jenny will live, Jenny will walk, Jenny will talk and Jenny will be totally normal again right now? You see I have the word of Jesus that Jenny will be totally normal! I have the word of Jesus that says by His strips Jenny was healed. I believe and I declare it to be and so it is, I have the word of Jesus on it!

Two different women over the years have delivered two words of knowledge from God to me. The first came about three years ago when I came across the scriptures about a sin unto death.

1Jn 5:16 If any man see his brother sin a sin which is not unto death, he shall ask, and he shall give him life for them that sin not unto death. There is a sin unto death: I do not say that he shall pray for it.

After reading this scripture I ask God to reveal the sin I needed to repent for. I waited and when I never heard from the Lord, I pleaded please God you know I choose You; only You have life! I knew God knew I would change and turn away from all wickedness if I just knew what I was doing wrong. After a couple days of asking the Lord about this scripture Jesus sent me a messenger.

The next morning a girl came to my camper and said I have never done this before but I believe I have a word from the Lord for you. She said I have known idea what this means to you but the word I keep hearing to tell you is "not unto death" I thanked her for being obedient to Jesus and for telling me the word God had for me. I immediately had the peace that surpasses all understanding in my heart. I continue to this day to speak those words over Jenny "Jesus said not unto death". Now I pray in thanks giving for I know that Jenny is healed and I know that Jenny will not die of this disease. Thank you Jesus for coming into my life and renewing my mind!

About a year and a half later Jenny and I were in a campground in Tennessee. They had a little church service in the campground so Jenny I went there for the service. It was a bright sunny morning and the service was under a pavilion with no walls. Jenny and I were late arriving, and as we approached the pavilion we were very quiet because we were in grass, (the wheel chair made no noise) but still somehow a lot of people turned around to see who came up behind them. I was kind of startled by them turning around because we made no noise and the preacher did not say anything or even look at us. Any way after the service I was walking Jenny back to our camper and some women stopped me to say why they turned around in the church service. They said even though it was a sunny day they felt the whole pavilion light up when we came. One woman said you glow with the love of Jesus in you. Then they walked away.

As Jenny and I continued to walk to our camper I had tears running down my face, I was crying so hard because I ask God to let me manifest His presents everywhere I go. I had my head down because I didn't want everyone to see me crying. There was another younger girl walking in front of us that suddenly turned around and ask if she could pray for Jenny. I replied sure, but before she started to pray, her two sons and husband that were behind us came walking up. As we talked for a moment I had reached my hand down and picked up Jenny's hand to hold it and with my other hand I was rubbing Jenny's face. This girl, the mother of the two boys said to her sons; "do you see why I said every time I see this man with his wife, I tell you boys I see Jesus". She continued to tell them, you see when you don't feel good Jesus is there with you holding your hand, Jesus will rub your head to comfort you and if you cannot walk Jesus will pick you up and carry you into your camper.

Then she started to pray for Jenny. In the middle of her prayer she stopped and said wow I just received a word for you. She went on to say "this one is to manifest the glory of God" after she finished her prayer I went to the camper and looked it up.

Joh 9:5 And as Jesus passed by, he saw a man which was blind from his birth. And his disciples asked him, saying, Master, who did sin, this man, or his parents, that he was born blind? Jesus answered, Neither hath this man sinned, nor his parents: but that the works of God should be made manifest in him. I must work the works of him that sent me, while it is day: the night cometh, when no man can work. As long as I am in the world, I am the light of the world.

As I read these scriptures I knew God was talking to me through His messengers again. Isn't it amazing that the creator of the universe has time to talk to me? We are all this special to God and if you're going through anything tough right now ask the creator to talk to you and He will comfort you also. This is why I tell everyone Jenny and I are so blessed. Jesus wants a relationship!!!

So when people look at me like I am crazy, I let them look because I know the truth of Jesus sets us free and the truth is God loves me and I will stand on these scriptures and I will see Jenny walking, talking, I know Jenny and I will have coffee with my brother Jesus! What a glorious day that will be! I command it to happen and it will happen because Jesus gave me His word on it. Jesus said anything I ask in faith I will receive that the Son may bring glory to the Father. Do you know the meaning of the words Father God? Father means to come forth from and God means the source of life. So when I go to MY FATHER GOD, I am going to the one from which we all come forth from and is the source of life. I mean I might as well go right to the source and I go to Him through my brother Jesus. I call that being blessed!

I know Jesus loves Jenny and I so much, He came to restore the relationship Adam lost by eating the fruit of the tree of Good and evil. Jesus came and restored that relationship so we walk and talk together 24/7. I have relationship with Jesus and my Father 24/7 and there is no better place to be then in the company of my Jesus and Father. If people want to say I am crazy I don't care, I know who I am and I know who loves me. Jesus said we will be peculiar and I love being what Jesus said I would be! I know Jesus said we can bring heaven to earth and I know I am already in Heaven because I know Jesus and my Father love me! Father God calls me His Son! Believing as a child in the word of God is rest and it is the only blessing I need! So to be blessed, I rest in God!

Yes I want Jenny healed and yes I am seeking her healing like I should because Jesus said by His strips we were healed, done deal! I also know that some people have said look how much closer you are to God because of this sickness in Jenny. I do not and will not ever believe that God puts sickness on people to bring them closer to Him. If you believe it is the will of God to put sickness on people to bring you closer to Him, you should never go to a doctor because you are asking the doctor to sin by going against the will of God!!! Also if sickness is the will of God then we should never fight it; we should just accept it, we should pray for more sickness so we can be in His will! You see how contrary to the Word of

God sickness is!!!! JESUS SAID HEAL SICKNESS, DON'T ACCEPT SICKNESS!!!!! Especially don't except it!!!

No one comes to God unless He calls us first. I don't see anywhere in the bible where Jesus called anyone and said if you do not come I will make you or your wife sick to get your attention. He might let a donkey talk to you but He never put sickness on anyone. Sickness is the work of the devil, not God. If you believe God put sickness on you, you will not or should not fight to get better, I mean after all, you think it is the will of God, right? Look at what Jesus calls sickness. Captivity, spirit of infirmity, bondage, and Jesus said He came to set the captives free, to free us from the bondage of sin and the spirit of infirmity. We in America have doctors that have a name forevery kind of sickness, but I believe all sickness is a spirit of infirmity and if you cast out an evil spirit of infirmity the sickness is gone, the pain is gone and health with life is back. Your health is renewed like the eagles. We can and should live in divine health every day. Devine health is ours for just believing.

I believe the first line of defense in sickness and disease is the church and not a hospital. If your faith is in doctors then by all means go to the doctor and live another day to have time to learn what a relationship with Jesus looks like. Learn what divine health is all about. The love of Jesus is so strong and it is His will to heal all!!!! Jesus will meet you at your faith level and even heal you through a doctor but when you get to heaven; wouldn't it be cool for Jesus to honor your faith like He did the men in Hebrews 11. I know when I get there I want to hear the words "well done my GOOD AND FAITHFUL SON; RON YOU BELIEVED ME!"

Faith is a substance like Jesus said but I believe the substance of faith is how much of your life did you live by the spirit of faith, the spirit of love, the spirit of truth, and how much did you believe in Jesus. Yes sin will be an issue for some but only for those that did not believe enough to repent. I really believe when you are standing before Jesus for judgment; how much you believed in his coming and dieing for us to have relationship with Him is going to be a bigger factor then how much you repented for sin. I mean when you have relationship with Jesus the devil flees and takes sin with him. Then if you do fall short of the glory of God you have an advocate and your advocate is JESUS AND JESUS LOVES YOU AND WILL FIGHT FOR YOU!!! When I sin I go to Jesus and thank Him for removing it and thank Him for restoring me back to Himself right away. I do not dwell on that failure I dwell on Jesus and His forgiveness for it is the truth of God that sets us free form sin. Just believe and watch the word of Jesus come true for you too! It is the truth that sets us free and Jesus is the truth!

Sin is so over ratted in church today. I know it is a big deal; sin can put me in hell for eternity so sin is a big deal! I said it is over ratted because they tell us we have to fight the devil all the time. Jesus said stand firm in His word and He does the battle. In other words I don't get up trying not to sin every day. Being Sin concusses is setting yourself up to sin because that is where your mind is. Trying not to sin every day brings us to a place where that is all you think about and after a while you will give in. If all you think about is sin, you will grow tired of fighting sin and you will back slide.

I don't get up and try not to sin, I get up to do the work of the kingdom by keeping my mind on Jesus, so I don't have to fight the devil because he is already defeated by Jesus. Jesus never fought the devil, he just ran over the devil because Jesus is like a speeding freight train on its way to Heaven. Jesus laid down some big tracks for us to follow! Let us all be a speeding freight train; destroying the works of the devil and full of the love of Jesus and by manifesting the Love of Jesus we will fill all our passenger cars to overflowing! Kingdom work is rewarding and uplifting, it is Joy beyond our understanding. Kingdom work is full of purpose so you don't grow weary and you won't back slide; in fact Jesus said I will give you rest. You will front slide right into the loving arms of Jesus for the biggest bear hug possible. It is a bear hug with a big well done my faithful Son who serves. Jesus is alive and well and He wants to flow through you and for you to manifest Him 24/7! MANIFESTING JESUS IS HOW NOT TO SIN!!! JESUS LOVES ME AND I KNOW IT SO I WIN!!!!

Remember when you fell in love with your girlfriend. You hoped with all your hope that she would fall in love with you. Your mind was on her 24/7. When she did fall in love with you, you relaxed and her love gave you peace in your heart to where your Joy was so full, you say I will marry you and take care of you the rest of your life. When you seek a relationship with Jesus as diligently as you seek a spouse, you will have the love of Jesus that surpasses all understanding and it adds new meaning to the words "take care of you." The Joy of God's love surpasses all our understanding! I believe in the loving joy of Jesus so I receive the loving joy of Jesus and I know Jesus loves me! That is truly the everlasting Joy of the Lord! I don't understand it but I sure in Joy it!!!

Most people are taught that receiving Jesus in to your heart and being saved is a bus ticket to heaven. I hear preachers say if you died tonight where would you spend eternity? They are selling your life insurance but instead of paying the premium with money you pay with good deeds. Then after a while you get tired of paying the premium because the policy is just words on paper and maybe you hear about the joy of the Lord but wonder what is that? Being Christian becomes a bunch of works. They hear of a life more abundant here on earth but wonder where is that? We really need to teach relationship with Jesus comes first. When you were seeking a wife, did you go to all her friends and do nice things for them hoping that somehow that would win her heart? No! You went right to her and pursued her, to win her heart.

A relationship with Jesus is pursuing Jesus first. You cannot have the Joy of the Lord without knowing Him. Jesus said bring heaven to earth, I tell you living with Jesus in you is bringing heaven to earth and then you can spread heaven around. Freely you received the Joy of knowing Jesus so freely you can spread the heavenly Joy of knowing Jesus around. Jesus is the ultimate motivator. His call to action was given to the 12 and then to the 70 and then the120 and now to you!!! Turn off the television and the computer and anything that distracts you form Jesus. Jesus told me to get the world out of the way and then you will hear what I have to say! Remember Jesus will not talk over the noise of the world, you have to set time a side to lesson and just believe.

The world says "don't get your hopes to high", you will be disappointed. Yet my bible tells me nothing is impossible for me with Jesus Christ living in me. I believe the word of God! My hopes are Jesus high!!

The world says to a new Christian, "you're on fire now but don't worry you will cool down" or some call it backsliding. To some degree in church today, it is almost expected for a new Christian to backslide. In the church today we pray to have new converts and yet Paul prayed unceasingly for the established church. The real attacks from the devil come after you are baptized and on fire. The devil wants to steel those new seeds before they root into your heart, and by us saying don't worry he will cool down is like pronouncing that on them. Encourage as Jesus encouraged, be light as Jesus was light, love as Jesus loved, live as Jesus lived, do the things you see your Father do and you to will have the Joy of the Lord. You will have converts that come to you because they will see the Jesus in you, the Joy in you, the Love in you and you will be contagious. People will want what you have! Just give them Jesus and be contagiously contagious! It's a good thing!

The world tells us to do this or to buy that and you will be happy. Jesus told me that happiness is the opposite of Joy. Happiness always comes from getting something for yourself or having something done for yourself and happiness is always momentary. Happiness is always about yourself! Joy is doing for others and Joy is sustainable forever!

The world says for us to do nice things for others and God will love you. That is backwards! Jesus didn't come to reap servants that are trying to please Him by works. Jesus came to reap Sons and Daughters who are in a faith relationship with Him! You serve others because of your intimate relationship with God! You do not serve others to have relationship with God! When you truly have relationship with Jesus and Father God the Joy of the Lord glows in you and flows out from you and people will want what you have. You bring people to God because of your relationship to God, you don't bring people to God to have a relationship with God! God is the light that people always go to! Let your relationship shine the love of Jesus to everyone you meet. Jesus told us to preach the gospel to the entire world so it must be possible for each one of us. You are in this world so preach right where you are. Jesus will use your light to be His light, right where you are. Just believe with God all things are possible and they are! You to can be a light because you have Jesus in you!

Life and light are called the Joy of the Lord! Read the life of Jesus and you will see the ultimate giver! Read His life and you will see Jesus gave of Himself to show people the love of His Father but you cannot give the love of the Father until you have relationship with Your Father! It is really hard to give away something you do not have. Life more abundant; life full of Joy; life of peace; life of rest; is impossible without knowing the one that makes all things possible. Please read about the possibilities and start a relationship with the one that makes all things possible! You cannot earn one and you cannot deserve one but I can guarantee you Jesus wants you to receive His relationship free of charge. Then Jesus said freely you received and freely you give. Give His love, give His peace, give His hope, give His trust, and you will light up the world. Most of all tell people how to have a relationship with Jesus.

Get the worldly out of the way and then you will hear what I have to say. Thank You From God! It is worth repeating! Get the impossible out of the way, by having relationship with the one that makes all things possible! Imagine the possibilities, imagine the Joy when you walk through life knowing Jesus the Son of God is your brother and Father God is your FATHER!!! Yes being a Christian is more than a bus ticket to heaven!

I'm going to close with this story form Jesus. Suppose your married and you have a young son and he was being bullied in school. Every night he asks his dad to talk to the teacher and so his dad does. The teacher said he will look out for Billy but he cannot be everywhere Billy is. So the three bullies knock Billy's books out of his hands while in the hallway. They still kick him around on the playground. So you decide to enroll Billy in carroty classes and boxing classes and a martial arts class. You want Billy to defend himself. In 6 months Billy has won all kinds of awards and is great in every class. In the fall when school starts again you are excited and you tell your wife this year will be different, Billy will show those three bullies a thing or two.

But Billy still comes home every night and complains about the bullies beating him up. Dad asks "son why don't you kick their tails, you know you can"

Billy says dad; I don't want to make them made at me, they might go and get more bullies.

In our new covenant with Jesus we have all the weapons we need to kick the devil back to hell. Jesus came and demonstrated these weapons; Jesus wrote down the instructions for us to pass on too future generations so the bullies will know they cannot mess with us who are in the Lord. We have the best defense system man kind has ever seen. Jesus is more then a buss ticket to heaven, He gives us power and authority and life without fear of bullies. Kicking out bullies in the name of Jesus is bringing heaven to earth.

Jesus said the only two requirements are to believe you received the power and authority and then use them. "I will show you my faith by my works" We should walk in power and authority! So when a bully called cancer comes on you and you are walking in power and authority; you will just command it to leave in the name of Jesus and believe by faith it is dead and gone. We give the bullies names like cancer or the flue; but there is really only three big bullies 1) kill 2) steel 3) destroy! Jesus called them devils and spirits of infirmity and He ran right over them. He put them under His feet. Are you getting the picture! We have power and authority and we are commanded to put the devil under our feet. So power up and use that God given authority. Give the devil some hell because he will give you a big dose of it if you let him!

This is the short version of sickness. Jesus and I are writing a longer one where we back up every statement we made with scripture. I know Jesus lives in me and so I can say we and I mean we, Jesus and me!

Jesus, Jenny and I love all of you!!!

April 6th, 2013

We arrived at Carrabelle Beach and form the minute we pulled in people were greeting us. Jenny seemed to enjoy being there also. I got our camper set up and Jenny and I went for a walk around the campground. We were only here for one week last year; so this year people wanted to say hello and see how Jenny was doing right away in case we were only here for one week again. There seemed to be a joy in the air and the joy picked Jenny up also. Jenny ate really good Saturday and I was sure glad to see her eating. I walked Jenny into the office and the girls greeted her with such love. I mean it was awesome being here again.

I cannot wait to go to church and see everyone there also. Being here is like coming home. I think Jenny knows where she is, we are camped right across from where we were the very first time we came here four years ago. I know from looking at Jenny and being with Jenny, she is excited and I believe the miracle of Jenny's health will happen real soon!

April 7th, 2013

I thought the love from fellow campers flowing at the campground was great but when we went to church today the love was truly overflowing. The joy at church Sunday seemed like heaven to us and really we are in heaven here. I received so many hugs and words of encouragement at church that I feel like a hero. Even the children were hugging and praying for us. I'm not sure what it will be like to go to heaven but I am pretty sure the people of Christian Carrabelle Center are role models. Thank you Jesus for getting us here and for making everyone so warm and wonderful!

After church our friend Ray, his father and mother in law, took Jenny and I out to eat. We had a whole year to catch up on. Ray has two children Ray Noel his daughter and Hunter his son so I wanted to hear how they were doing also. We were in the restaurant a long time. Other people greeted us and I was beginning to feel like a celebrity.

The only down side on Sunday was Jenny seemed overly tired and did not eat much. I assumed Jenny was tired from all the excitement Saturday. I took her back to the camper and held her on my lap. I truly love holding her on my lap, Jenny seems so comfortable and so restful. I have to thank my Jesus for this comfort and the enjoyment of holding Jenny on my lap. In just a short time she woke up and ate pretty good but still not as much as I would have liked. After feeding her I set her on my lap again and Jenny slept some more. As Jenny was sleeping I started thinking about her eating habits and trying to figure out when she started slowing down on her eating.

I looked on the calendar to see when Jenny's last seizure was? On January 29th Jenny had a long seizure and it took her about two days to return to base line. It came to me that Jenny has not been eating regularly since January 29th. Some days she would eat everything I gave her and other days she would hardly eat at all. Another difference I was noticing in Jenny was her drinking. She was not drinking as much either. For a long time Jenny did not seem to recognize a straw until I put some of her drink in her mouth. Now she doesn't seem to recognize the fact I want her to drink. When I put the straw in her mouth she was trying to chew it instead drinking through it. I really miss Jenny's excitement about the food I prepare for her. I know my Jesus will make the food she is getting everything she needs so I just praise Him for this miracle also!!!

April 8th, 2013

Monday the 8th Jenny and I were sitting under our awning when a man came up and said Hi Bill, now is Jenny doing? She is doing great but my name is Ron, he started laughing and said no wonder I couldn't find anyone who remembered you two. His name was Don and his wife was Val. They had camped here four years ago for one night. Their big motor home was brand-new and had a broken drawer so I fixed it. They have been coming every year since and hoped they would see us again and find out how Jenny was doing. Now we all ended up here at the same time, how cool is that? They are from Canada. Their daughter and five month old granddaughter who are also from Canada flue down to spend a ten-day holiday here with them. Jenny and I are blessed to see them again and then Jesus put some icing on the cake with letting us meet their daughter Leah and her baby girl.

I gave Don a copy of Jenny's book to read and he read it in two nights, I really loved hearing Don's opinion on things because he has such a net way of expressing himself. Together Don and Val have traveled around the United States four times in four years. They have also traveled to different countries and in their travels they have helped many, many people.

They are like missionaries but without organized church backing them up or as Don put it holding them back. Don talked about their journey and shared how they sought out the back roads in the countries they visited. They would find needy families and fulfill their needs. Don's special way of expressing himself carries over to the special way his big heart expresses his love for mankind and the people that most people would overlook. Jenny and I hold a special place in our heart for them and I know Jesus does too! Jesus I love you and love the good people you put in our path.

In the bible Jesus refers to life as a vapor of time. Our vapors will be gone like the wind, as Jesus said you don't know from where it came or where it shall go. The cool thing about us vapors is when we get out from behind the television or computer and let the Lord led our wind, no one will know from where we came or where we go but they will know we have been there. Make your vapor count by letting your love of the Lord show. To let your love of Jesus show, simply let your love go to all you met along your journey.

April 11ᵗʰ, 2013

On Thursday I called our three children and told them about the down turn in Jenny. I also called Jenny's birth mom (Rosemary) to give her a little heads up about Jenny. Rosemary lives with her sister and two nieces, Carolyn one of the nieces, answered the phone and immediately upon hearing about Jenny ask me if Jenny was in the camper with me. I said yes. She told me Jenny needed to be in a hospital. I ask her how she could make a judgment call like that in a thirty second conversation. She started screaming so I just hung up the phone. She left me four or five nasty messages, then she left one saying she called adult protection services to report that I was not taking care of my wife.

For the past six or seven years I have visited Jenny's mother Rosemary once a year usually around Christmas so Rosemary could at least see and spend some time with one of her daughters. Rosemary had 9 children and all were in foster homes or adopted. In my heart I felt no connection to Rosemary and I know Jenny never did either.

I did feel as though it was the right thing to do and I considered it an act of kindness to visit her. Rosemary seemed to enjoy these visits with us and I really think Jenny did also. I looked forward to them because there is a joy that comes from doing the will of my Father. The worst part of visiting them was there are five people living together in a small house and they all smoke and there was no ventilation at all. The smoke would get to my throat really quick and I figured it was getting to Jenny's also, so we only stayed about a half hour, and then we would leave. I will say out of a curtsey they did not smoke while Jenny and I were there.

The message from adult protection services was very upsetting. To think after all these years of taking care of my Jenny, I would be under investigation and to think the investigation was

111

triggered by a 45 second phone call is just beyond belief to me. Just the thought of someone taking Jenny away made me sick to my stomach.

April 12th, 2013

On Friday morning I did call Carolyn and ask her not to call anymore. I told her I would call again if there were any changes in Jenny but I did not want her calling me anymore. I said anyone that would try to take my wife away from me doesn't need to call me anymore. She knows Jenny and I have been married for 40 years and she knows I have loved Jenny and for the past 9 to 10 years taken care of Jenny 24/7. I ask her not to call anymore.

Friday afternoon I did receive a message from the police department in Pierce Township, wanting to know where Jenny and I were because they had been to our old address and no one was home. When I called back they said the investigating officer had gone home for the day and would not be back until Wednesday the 17th.

Upon hearing about his mom, Ronnie left home that night to come see Jenny. He had to work around his work schedule so he drove 14 hours, stayed 5 hours and drove 14 hours back home. It was the best 5 hours I have ever spent with Ronnie. Our time together went so fast. We talked about faith, Jenny's healing, God's will, and living a God centered life. I cried when he left the camper because our time was so short and the camper seemed so empty. Just seeing him here and seeing the love for his mom and I; seeing his concern and knowing he is alright with the decisions I'm making was a wonderful reassurance. Naturally I love our children but it is an awesome thing to have mutual respect.

After Ronnie left I started pondering this journey I'm on and how my children never said a word when I spent literally every bit of money I had trying to pay the house payment and pay the medical bills. They never second-guessed me when I borrowed against the house time and time again to pay the medical bills. They never voiced an opinion when I sold the business and when that money ran out they let me sell the house without any opposition.

When I told them I was buying a $10,000 camper to live in, I know they were questioning my judgment but kept their questions to their selves. Now looking back at those decisions I realize what a blessing it was not to have any interference from them. Even after the first motor home I bought caught on fire and was totaled they didn't voice opposition to me buying another one. They really have held their tongs and just let me be in control of their mother's life. I mean taking Jenny on the road in an old camper probably didn't look like the best decision to them. One big repair bill on the camper or a medical bill could have wiped out my finances and then I could have been a burden to them. I thank my Jesus that didn't happen and I thank my Jesus for their understanding and for their quite tongs.

On Friday afternoon our friends John and Patty came down from Crawfordsville to spend a long weekend with us. They are so nice and told me not to plan any meals because they had them for us. I know they were shocked that Jenny had changed so much in the last year, but they were so helpful and so loving. I thank God for them being here and for their loving, caring way of helping in any way they could. Jenny and I were so blessed to be with them.

April 13th, 2013

Patty and John and Jenny and I spent a lot of time together and even went to the beach on Saturday. Jenny really enjoyed hearing the waves and feeling the sun. You could tell Jenny loved being by the gulf, because she actually tried to smile. I liked being by the gulf because she was so calm and content. It was good to see Jenny so happy and content lessoning to the waves. I was hoping Jenny's appetite would pick up after being on the beach that afternoon but it did not.

Jason arrived Saturday night and we had a great visit also. Jason had a hard time looking at his mom. Her face is drawing in and she is so skinny. You can see all her bones; she really is hard to look at. While talking Jason ask me what would I say to someone that has earnestly prayed for over a year to find a better job and has not found one. I was not prepared for his question so I said out loud "Holy spirit how should I answer" immediately I heard the answer. I told Jason the bible teaches me it is possible for you to pray amiss.

Jas 4:3 Ye ask, and receive not, because ye ask amiss, that ye may consume it upon your lusts.

You see Jesus sees the whole picture and if the things you are asking for do not line up with the word of God or His will, He might not answer that prayer. Then Jesus gave me this example.

Let's say Jason you are super rich and you have a son who asks you for a new corvette on his 16th birthday next month. You have the means to just write a check and your son knows it. You start thinking to yourself; a corvette is way too much car for a 16year old. You desire to make him happy but you realize if he had this powerful car, he might have an accident and hurt someone or worse he could end up dead. You think this car he wants could take him away from me and so in your wisdom you tell him you will not buy him a corvette for his 16th birthday, but when you turn 25 years old if you are mature enough I will buy it for you then.

I believe God is like the wise man that did not buy his son the corvette. You see God sees the big picture also, when we pray amiss we are asking God for something that might take us further from God or we might hurt ourselves with it or we might kill ourselves with it. I believe it is the desire of God to have a personal relationship with us, toys like campers, motor cycles, boats etc. can take our mind off Jesus and become a lust or sought after items that take us away from Jesus instead of bring us closer to Jesus.

When we pray I believe God answers all prayers but maybe the answer is not what we believe Him for so we say our prayers are not answered; when in reality we are just not lessoning. The boy that wanted a corvette might even be mad at his dad for not letting him have a corvette, but we can see the wisdom in the dad's decision. If we just give God some quite time we will see His wisdom also! To give God quite time is one of the biggest gifts you can give your Father and in that quite time you will hear form the creator and you will be astonished at what Jesus wants to talk about!!!

The boy Jason knows prayed for a job for over a year. Then when he didn't get a new job he said I'm going to stop praying. That also reveals his heart. You see he was not looking for a relationship; he was just trying on God. If he gets what he wants from God then God is good, but if he doesn't then he said I will stop praying. The only reason he prayed was to get what he wanted. He was not seeking a lasting relationship with God; he just wanted what he wanted form God. Jesus doesn't really ask for much except a little of your time here on earth. Please give God your time and have a relationship that will last for eternity.

When Jason left the camper again I felt emptiness in my spirit and in the camper again. I haven't had time to think about it but I think I had wanted our children to experience the love of the people of Carrabelle and for my friends to meet them. Like the vapor of life, you cannot hold in your hand or capture in a physical

116

place. You can put it in your heart and like the word of Jesus; there you can recall it any time. Seeing both our boys here was a real treat for Jenny and I and having someone on one time with them has blessed my Spirit forever!

I talked to Heidi and she said she made her peace with mom when we were in California in 2010. So she did not come. I know Heidi is really okay with the decisions I am making for her mom and I think she has a peace about that!

April 14th, 2013

Jenny and I went to church; Pastor Don had another great message. Our friends loved on Jenny and prayed for her. A guy named Kim and his grandson (Tyler) earnestly prayed for a long time. In my heart I know Jenny is healed and I know all these prayers are going to be answered real soon.

Jenny's breathing seemed labored and a couple people said the oak pollens were really bad this year. I was able to suction Jenny's nose and that seemed to help her breathing a lot.

Jenny's eating is getting worse. This happened about a month ago also! All I did then was blend her food in a food processor and I was still able to get food in her. It only lasted a couple days and praise God Jenny started eating again. This time I'm doing the same thing but Jenny is not eating much. I have tried her favorite foods and nothing is working. Kim from church brought over some protein powder and Pediatric drink. I'm getting some in Jenny and she seems to like them both. I continue to pray, I ask the Lord to bless our food and to make the amount or the quantity that Jenny is getting the right amount for her. Thank you Jesus for making every little bit I get in Jenny the right amount to sustain Jenny's life until the healing manifests which has to happen real soon.

April 15th, 2013

Monday morning we hung out with Patty and John. They took us to a restaurant for lunch and although the food was very good Jenny didn't eat much. Monday afternoon Patty and John went to the gulf to fish so Jenny and I went for a walk in the roadside park across form the campground. We met a really nice lady and talked to her about Jesus for about an hour. She seemed to be very receptive and wanted a book about Jenny. When she left she seemed to have a little more zip in her step, I know I did! I think she said she was 80 years old but very spry.

Jenny and I went back to the camper and I did get Jenny to eat a little and she drank a lot which was very good. The bad news is by about nine o'clock Jenny's discharge from her nose turned green. It made feeding her even harder. That evening I called pastor Don's wife Lisa, who is a nurse, to ask her about Jenny. I told Lisa about the discharge from her nose being green and Lisa said Jenny has an infection and should be on antibiotics. So on her recommendation I took Jenny to the emergence room. Lisa also recommended I think about calling hospice. I told her I would.

On the way to the emergence room Jenny fell asleep and her arms relaxed, they had been folded across her chest for months now. When I got to the hospital which was only about 18miles with no traffic lights, in other words an easy drive. I carried Jenny into the emergence room and the nurses were not busy thank you Jesus. The nurse checked Jenny and reported to the Doctor.

When Dr. Conrad came in he asks Jenny to lean forward and take a deep breath. Naturally Jenny did not respond and I ask the doctor if he knew what picks disease was. He looked at me and very true fully said "when the nurse told me I had a patient with picks disease, I remembered a couple questions about Picks disease on an exam I took a 30 years ago." He said I did stop and look it up on the computer before I came in, I just didn't know what stage she was in. Dr. Conrad ordered an x-ray of Jenny's lungs. After checking them he said Jenny has the start of pneumonia and added her lungs are still working at 100% on room air and that was a very good sign. He ordered a shot and gave me a prescription.

When the nurse came in she ask me to roll Jenny on her side so she could give Jenny the shot in the muscle mass, I told her there is no mussel there. After examining Jenny's bottom she said I will ask the doctor if I can give her the antibiotics in her vain.

A little while later Dr. Conrad came back into the room and ask me how long have you been taking care of Jenny? I told him. He said he could admit Jenny for a couple days to give me a break. I said thank you doctor but I want Jenny to be with me in the camper and I really do not need a break.

Pastor Don whom had come to the hospital to be with Jenny and I said Doctor I have known Ron for four years; no one knows how he does it but I can tell you he does not want or need a break. Doctor Conrad then wrote his personal phone number on a piece of paper and said I could call any time day or night and he would do everything possible to help Jenny and I. What a blessing; God never ceases to amaze me. Thank You Jesus for the nice people you put in our path.

The good news was Jenny and I were on our way home and the hospital visit was less than two hours. Thank you Jesus! Dr. Conrad did recommend Hospice be called and so we set up for them to come Tuesday morning.

April 16th, 2013

Patty and John left on Tuesday morning to go back to Crawfordsville. It sure was nice having them here and it was really nice not to cook all weekend. They have been good friends since we met four years ago. Thank you both for being here and helping so much. I know Jenny enjoyed the beach last Saturday and that would not have been possible if Patty and John didn't help get Jenny there.

Also on Tuesday I had time to think about how nice it was for Doctor Conrad to give me his personal cell phone number. I tell everyone Jenny and I are so blessed and God keeps blessing us with nice people in our lives. It was totally above the call of duty for Pastor Don to come to the hospital that late and it was above the call of duty for Dr. Conrad to give me his personal Cell phone number. Again THANK YOU JESUS FOR THESE BLESSINGS.

I also want to add that Jenny's personal doctor at home is also a friend that has been to our house for dinner and yet I don't have his personal cell phone number. Jenny has seen the same neurologist for ten years and I don't have his personal cell phone number either. I am not trying to put down these two doctors in any way; I only bring this up to say why I think it was so far above the call of duty for Dr. Conrad to give me his. Again thank you Jesus for the nice people you put in our path all the time.

Before we went to the hospital that night Lisa had also ask me to consider calling hospice, so I told her I would. At the hospital Dr. Conrad also suggested it, and there was a hospice nurse working at the hospital who talked to me before I left. Hospice started coming Tuesday morning.

Lisa was right, they are a big help and I am glad they are here. They all know I believe Jenny is healed and they also know how God has guided my footsteps all the way along this Journey. If they think I am crazy they respectively and professionally have kept those comments to themselves.

The antibiotics worked and Jenny is breathing better. Hospice ordered oxygen just in case we would need it. As it turns I put Jenny on oxygen that night for a couple hours. . I really did not know if Jenny needed oxygen but it seemed to relax her and she slept better. I started having her on oxygen part of every day. When nurse Diane came she would check Jenny's lungs and said they were at 96%. Her eating picked up after she started breathing better. And I was able to get three 8oz bottles of pediatric solution and 8oz of insure in Jenny. Jenny ate about half a can of red beets.

That night I unpacked Jenny's bowels and she had a good one. These are big blessings from My Jesus and I love Him for being so good to Jenny and I. Even though Jenny ate well today I am excited because I know Jenny's miracle has to be close. She is very very skinny and bony. It really is hard to look at her so thin and frail looking. I truly cannot wait to see her healed. God has blessed me a million times and more with every kind of blessing possible, I thank you Jesus and Father God for these blessings!!! I am getting really excited to see the miracle of Jenny's healing.

I believe I had to call hospice in for a reason. They checked Jenny for bed sours and could not find any. They were totally amazed. I told them it has to be a gift from Jesus because I cannot stop bed sours form coming no matter what I do here on earth except I do pray against them. Another blessing form my Jesus. Thank You Jesus!!!!

April 17th, 2013

Nurse Diane came and saw me scrubbing Jenny's teeth.

I have to put the sealed end of a sharpie felt marker in between Jenny's teeth to hold her mouth open to allow me to scrub the inside of her teeth. The sharpie pen is soft enough that it does not hurt her teeth and yet hard enough to keep her mouth open to allow me to clean her teeth. I use the sharpie felt marker while cleaning the roof of her mouth. If God did not tell me these tricks I don't know what I would do. Nurse Diane said that was really a cool way to keep Jenny's mouth open while cleaning her teeth.

I totally give all the credit to God for these tips on how to take care of Jenny because I don't think of them on my own. I simply ask God I need to clean Jenny's teeth and the next thing I know I have an answer. I ask the nurse how do people that don't believe in God handle something like this. She said that is easy, they put the sick person in a home and they go on with their lives. To me that is so sad because God has blessed with everything I need and more to take care of Jenny. I know not everyone has the desire to take care of their loved one so I thank you Jesus for the desire to take care of Jenny and for making it so easy.

A bright side to the nurses coming is they check Jenny from head to toe and found no bed sours. Nurse Diane said it is almost impossible for Jenny not to have bed sours. She estimated Jenny's weight to be around 60 pounds. She said you must be taking really good care of Jenny for her not to have bed sours. I said I give the credit to God because I cannot stop bed sours form being on Jenny. Nurse Diane said you and Jesus are a team aren't you? I said we are a team and the cool thing is Jesus loves us like no one else can love us!!! Without my Jesus there is no team.

I told Nurse Diane, I have noticed Jenny's feet swell a little during the day but come back to normal at night when they are elevated. She said that is fairly normal and that we should keep checking them, but as long as they come back to normal at night that is good. Again thank you Jesus.

In the afternoon I received a phone call from adult protective agency in Cincinnati. The investigating officer asked about Jenny and where we were. I told her, we have lived in the motor home for over four years. I gave her the names of Jenny's doctors and how long we have been seeing them. She ask me a couple questions, then I told her hospice was coming to the camper every day and she ask for their phone number. I believe when the investigating officer heard that hospice was involved, she was satisfied that all was well and Jenny was getting proper care. I thank you Jesus for telling Lisa to have me call in hospice and for giving Lisa the wisdom to see I needed them.

April 18th, 2013

The hospice Chaplin came today, we had a real nice talk about Jesus and our beliefs. I could of talked all day but

Linda the human resource lady came and the Chaplin left.

Linda gave me a list of papers I need to have on hand. Like power of attorney, medical power attorney, birth certificate, living will and our marriage certificate. I called Jason, gave him the list, told him these papers are all in the fireproof safe and he faxed them to me. Thank you Jason!

Linda also wanted to know what funeral arrangements have I made. I said none because Jenny is going to be healed by Jesus. I knew what she wanted, so I told her Jenny and I have been organ donors for about thirty-five years now. I showed her Jenny's state ID card with the little mark that designates this. Linda said Jenny does not weigh enough to be an organ donor. Linda said she would find out if the science labs would take her for research?

Linda asks if I wanted Jenny resuscitated, I told her no! She said that was easy. I told her I don't want man to resuscitate her because if they were successful Jenny would still be the same. I said I want Jesus to resuscitate Jenny so she will be healed. Later while talking to Nurse Diane; she said that was a good decision because Jenny is so small the procedure for resuscitating Jenny would really hurt her.

After Linda left I noticed there was some white stuff in the roof of Jenny's mouth, so I called Nurse Diane and she came over and gave me some special sponges on a stick called Den Tips. I cleaned that white stuff out of Jenny's mouth but there was more the next day. I never noticed it before so I guess it is just something to be cleaned every day. I don't know where it comes from.

April 19th, 2013

Jenny seems really tried to day, I have been trying to get her to eat but there doesn't seem to be any interest. Jenny's tong isn't moving her food to the back of her mouth. I know I have prayed about this before and Jesus has always made it work but this time it seems worse. I am literally watching Jenny shrink. She keeps losing weight. I have blended everything I can think of and Jenny is just not eating. Dearest Jesus please show me what to do. Jesus, You always come through and so I am just going to rest knowing Jenny and I are in your hands. I know for sure Jenny's condition is going to be healed because you say so in your word and that is all I need. Thank You Jesus for your encouragement from years ago when you said "this one is for the glory of God" I believe your word and Jenny's going to be healed for the glory of my Jesus!!!

Nurse Diane came by so I told her, Jenny's tong will not move food from the front of her mouth to the back so feeding her food is not happening. Nurse Diane said I should probably start using thickener for her drinks to keep Jenny from chocking and aspirating. I told her I can get liquids down Jenny without her chocking. The problem is food doesn't move to the back of her mouth, how will thickened drinks move back? So I have been giving her liquids and praying they go down the right path and guess what they are. I thank my Jesus they are and Jenny is not chocking and I continue to pray for her tong to start working again, and thank you Jesus it will!

Today while nurse Diane was here Jenny got real fidgety, Diane ask if I thought Jenny was in pain. I said I don't think so; I was at our table doing some paper work for hospice. I stopped what I was doing and went over to pick Jenny up and put her on my lap so we could snuggle up together. Jenny melted into me as usual and went to sleep. Diane smiled and said that is wonderful, it is better then any drug we could give her. Some times while holding Jenny I have a CD playing the word of God. I forget to talk to her because I am lessoning to the word of God. Jenny will wake up, try to look around and if I don't start talking she gets upset. As soon as I start talking or singing to her, Jenny relaxes and goes back to sleep. God is still blessing me with Jenny recognizing my voice and my touch. How do you thank Jesus enough for all these blessings?

When I have Jenny on my lap I know for a fact I am in heaven! Jenny is the sweetest most delightfully precious present God can give me and He does so every day. Thank You Jesus for these precious moments, I only hope when Jenny is healed that we don't get so busy that we miss this special time with you! Thank you Jesus for these special times with You and for my Jenny too!!! Jesus you always go exceedingly beyond anything I ask for and I thank You!

I know I am blessed to have this awesome relationship with Jesus and I thank You Jesus for every day with you also. Our relationship is so awesome; I believe in you and you alone so I rest even in my circumstances because You alone are the one who can make Jenny eat, drink, swallow, breath, and love! Thank you Jesus for your continual flow of blessings.

When I showed Nurse Diane how I was giving Jenny liquids she told me how to use a syringe to put liquids in the side of Jenny's mouth, she said this new way will help her swallow the liquids faster and better. I tried it and it is working. I can get insure and Pedialite down Jenny a lot faster. It is not food but it is something. Thank you Jesus for sending your help through Diane. Yes that is right I am hearing from my Jesus through Diane. I just have to recognize Jesus is talking through the people He is putting in my life right now. Thank You Jesus!!!!

Diane said she was going to Wal-Mart Saturday and ask if she could pick anything us for me while there. I said I need replacement toothbrush heads for our Sonicare tooth brush. I gave her an old brush head one to match the new ones up with. After Diane left I thanked my Jesus again for all the nice people He has put in my life.

The girl came to observe me bathing Jenny, she said you seem to have a joy about you and I said I do because I have been praying for ten years for a miracle and it has to be very close! I mean Jenny has not had solid food or any food for days. To me that is already a miracle of life. Right now she is asleep, barely breathing but I am able to have her swallow liquid. The good news is Jenny is alive and loves to be held by me, if that is not a miracle then what is. What a blessing from my Jesus to be able to love Jenny and hold Jenny and feel her tiny little body get so comfortable by just being held and loved.

When hospice ask me if I wanted someone to bath Jenny, I told them to come and observe me bathing Jenny so the hospice person could tell me if she had any special helpful tips to make Jenny more comfortable while I bath her. She observed and I have to tell you it was the worse shower I have ever given Jenny.

I stood Jenny up in the shower and started to bath her when Jenny's legs started giving out. I tried to set Jenny on the little seat in the shower but she kept sliding off the seat. I stood her up again and held her up with one hand and at the same time I had to help hold Jenny up with my head against her body to steady her and I finished bathing her in this awkward position. It was truly upsetting to me because bathing can be a problem but this time bathing Jenny became a nightmare. Shortly after I dressed her the girl left and I settled down. Jenny was exhausted and slept for a long time on my lap. I have never had that much trouble bathing Jenny but her legs kept giving away, at least Jenny is clean and I love her clean. I love and praise my Jesus that again Jenny still has no bed sours.

April 20th, 2013

Jenny woke up kind of happy today. I don't really know how to explain that but Jenny just seems happy. It is such a good thing to see. I thank you Jesus and I praise you that Jenny will drink and eat today. As the day progressed I did manage to get liquids down Jenny and some of our laundry done. We have been in the camper for over a week and Jenny seems to be doing very good today so I took her outside and she set in our lawn chair while I grilled some hot dogs.

Some new people were camping next to us. After talking to them for a while I gave him Jenny's book. Sometime latter his 17 year old daughter (Kaolin) came over and said her mother told her about Jenny's book and she ask if she could have a book for herself. I gave her one and she started reading it also.

Saturday evening Kaolin came over with her dad and we all had a nice time talking about the Lord. It was really nice to see them and to be able to speak into their lives. I was feeding Jenny some liquid while Kaolin observed. She seemed to be very moved and almost cried. We really enjoyed talking.

A round ten o'clock Kaolin and her dad left to go back to their camper. Jenny was asleep on the couch so I decided to do some more laundry. While walking back from the laundry I heard from Jesus, He wanted me to give Kaolin a couple teachings. I went to the car to get the teachings out of the file I keep on the back seat. I went to her camper because the lights were still on. As I walked around to the other side of their camper to knock on their door, I saw Kaolin was setting at the picnic table reading Jenny's book. I gave her the new teachings and she thanked me with a hug. Again she was very receptive! I hope and pray that our paths cross again someday.

April 21st, 2013

I got Jenny up, gave her a shower, I was able to get some liquid in her and we went to church. Don's message was really great and I needed to hear it. Jenny didn't seem to want to stay in the wheel chair so I took her out and held her. For about a half hour or so Jenny was asleep in my arms and real content, and then she started stiffing out. I could not get her comfortable no matter what I did. I finally just took Jenny out of church and to the car, I just could not get her comfortable in church so we went home to our camper. I held Jenny on the couch and she looked like she found her long lost friend. I held her until she fell asleep. Our neighbor Kaolin and her parents had packed up and gone already.

The rest of the day I spent feeding Jenny liquids. Jenny slept a lot Sunday but when she was awake she did drink some. I prayed to Jesus and talked to Jesus about the decisions I was making about Jenny's body. I wanted her to know I was fully expecting her to live because I knew she could hear my conversations with hospice. I told her it was no different than when we made the decision to donate our bodies to be organ donors 35 years ago. We were not expecting to die right away but we were making future plans. Now because of our circumstances I was making more future plans.

I don't know how much of that Jenny understood but I felt if Jenny understood what my conversations with hospice were about I needed to make it clear these plans were all in the future. One thing I wanted to make crystal clear was my intensions were for her to be healed 100% by my Jesus! I believe Jesus let Jenny understand because Jesus in his word says in all your getting get understanding.

Pro 4:7 Wisdom is the principal thing; therefore get wisdom: and with all thy getting get understanding.

I believe wisdom is the understanding of wisdom! I believe Jenny did understand all the paper work I had to do for hospice was necessary for their records but I was not making plans for Jenny to die, I was simply going through the formalities of their paper work. I rest in You Jesus to make that perfectly clear to my Jenny and I know since it is a desire of my heart to have her understand; Jenny does understand!!! Thank you Jesus for your perfect love that takes away our burdens. I have Your perfect love in my heart and I know Jenny does too so I rest in it. Praise you Jesus for coming and dying here on earth to restore our ability to have an awesome relationship with you.

As I set here with my little Jenny on my lap, I really want to cry my eyes out. I want to scream my lungs out but I know these things are fleshly desires and would not accomplish anything. These fleshly things would upset Jenny and so I know they really would only make things worse. Again I am thankful that Jenny is here with me and the two of us can still enjoy each other's company. What a blessing form Jesus and what a Joy I have knowing Jesus is the best comforter and the only comforter that can make any sense of this!!!!

April 22nd-24th, 2013

Jenny spent a lot time sitting on my lap sleeping. I had scriptures playing 24/7, bathing Jenny and I in the word of God. I am so thankful for the word of God in my life. Some of the time while holding Jenny on my lap, as she slept my mind would drift back to the past and how we raised our children. I would think about the good times and want to cry. I thought about our vacations with our little family of three, and how all five of us slept in the tent together. I loved when all of us were together, the love we shared, the time we spent on vacations were some of the happiest times to think about. I talked to Jenny about those times because I didn't want her to forget them. Jenny seemed to lesson even though she was asleep for most of those conversations. Jesus you are the greatest and I will never forget your love and how you let me be the recipient of your love flowing through my Jenny.

I admit that crying about old times is probably a sign of giving up. I know that hospice said if Jenny starts crying it is a sign of chocking but I believe Jenny was thinking about our past life together and our happiest times, like I was. We have been and are so blessed, our children are all doing pretty well and they are blessing also. I believe Jenny cried during our talks because of the happiness we shared and are sharing right now. Thank You Jesus for all these happy memories and for the Joy they bring, I know Jenny enjoys them also!

On Tuesday I decided to take one of Jenny's books to Dr Conrad. I loaded her in the car and off we went. Jenny seemed to know she was in the car and going somewhere. Jenny's little face seemed to show some excitement. We drove the 18 miles to the hospital and dropped off the book. There is an IGA store right there also so I took Jenny in the wheel chair and we went shopping. Jenny did great sitting up, I only needed a couple things so we were not in the store long. I set Jenny back in the car and we headed home. I didn't realize it then but this trip really exhausted Jenny, on the way home Jenny fell asleep, in about 25minutes we were home. I carried Jenny in the camper and sat her on the couch, she woke up for a couple minutes, long enough to get her to take a drink, and then she slept for two and a half hours.

All three days were spent feeding liquids to Jenny and she did really well but she continued to lose weight and that was very hard to look at. Her legs were becoming skin and bones, her arms also were skin and bones, actually her whole body was skin and bones. I could not seem to get enough liquid down Jenny to keep weight on her. I ask God to bless what I was getting down Jenny and for God to make it enough. My life, my time, my everything for the past ten years has been spent taking care of Jenny and getting to know Jesus in a personal way. I would not change one minute and I thank you Jesus for every one of those minutes because they are all precious to me also.

A while ago I was talking to a guy going through a divorce. It was an ugly divorce and the things they did to each other, I mean the hate, the hurtfulness, the tearing each other up right in front of the children and them both using the children as ponds to hurt each other. To me that was way worse than what I'm going through. I never suffered rejection and hate towards me from my loved one. In fact our love grew through our trial. We never doubted each other, in fact we prayed to stay together, our love stayed in tack and in forty years of marriage we are more in love now than anyone I know. I have so much to be thankful for, I have really big blessings from my Jesus and the best part of knowing Jesus is knowing He will never leave us or forsake us. I bet anyone that has gone through a divorce would like a guarantee like that from the love of their life. The cool thing is they can have love like that if they just believe the one that said I cannot lie and if they can believe Jesus meant it!!!

Jenny and I are more blessed then anyone I know. Our love never faltered, we both have known the love of Jesus and there is nothing better than knowing Jesus loves you. Someday soon Jenny will be healed and we will talk about every day of this journey, we will walk, hold hands and know the best is yet to come. I believe Jenny will know everyone we have met along the way. I believe everyone will be totally surprised by what she remembers.

April 25th, 2013

Today Jesus had something special for me because I woke up and had my coffee with Jesus when I heard Jenny stir. That was really good news because the last couple days I have had to wake Jenny up. Today Jenny woke up on her own. Thank you Jesus! I changed her, bathed her and got Jenny something to drink. Jenny always liked orange juice in the morning so instead of her insure I gave Jenny some orange juice. She really did good drinking but fell asleep in between sips. I could gently move her and she came awake again to drink some more.

It is hard to believe it was over thirty years ago when Jenny and I decided to be organ donors. We have that indicated on our driver's license for years and it is on Jenny's state I D. Linda the hospice social worker said now Jenny does not weigh enough to be an organ donor. She checked and found a place called Science Care that might want Jenny's body to study because of the picks disease. I know Jenny has always been a giver of everything all her life and so now she will be one after death also. I enrolled Jenny in to the program today. There were some painful decisions to make, it really hurts to be talking about her death and planning her death when I know Jenny is healed. All this planning is not necessary because Jenny is healed and the hospice nurses will see that real soon. I know it is just a formality that we must go through so I do. Kind of like when they ask Jesus to pay taxes and he did to fulfill there formality.

About two o'clock this afternoon, Linda, came for her visit. She had the information about Science Care. We did the interview on the phone. I had three options to consider about Jenny's body.

- First; they keep Jenny's body for six weeks and after they harvest what they need, they cremate the rest and send the ashes to me.

- Second; they keep Jenny's body for three years and then cremate the remains and send the ashes to me. The girl on the phone said they learn a lot more in the three years.

- Third; they keep the body indefinitely and learn even more.

I chose the third because Jenny was always a 100% giver and I did not want to change the way Jenny lived after her death, so I could have a bottle of ashes.

There were other decisions to be made and none of them were easy. It is hard to talk about these things while Jenny is sitting there, I know she can hear and I believe she understands.

After Linda left I sat with Jenny and told her again how we made the plans to be organ donors thirty years ago, now I am making plans for the future but that does not mean these plans will happen anytime soon.

Thursday was a good day for getting drinks down Jenny and scrubbing Jenny's teeth. Jenny's urine was not as strong and she filled three pampers. Now that was a miracle!

I ask Jesus when I was finished enrolling Jenny why I should even go through the enrolment, because Jenny is healed and it seemed so contradictory to Your word. Then Jesus asks me if you were thirsty would you get up and get a drink of water or would you sit and wait for me to get you one? I said I would get myself one. Jesus said why would you get yourself a drink of water when you know I am your provider, why don't you just sit and wait for me to get you one? I said because you did provide me with water and you did provide all my needs but I must still use my free will and decide to get the water you provided for me. I said I think I understand Jesus. I am in the world and I understand I have to do things like get my own glass of water. I understand I have to pay taxes and live by the rules of my government. I guess I have to be understanding of the non-believers and play by the rules they set, even when they don't understand the healing power of my Jesus.

Any way Jenny is enrolled in the science care program and those hard decisions are finished. If Jesus decides to take her home to her final reward then her body will not just go in some hole in the ground and rote. The scientist can study it and maybe find a better way to help fight picks disease in the future. After 40 years of marriage I can say without a doubt that Jenny would have made the same decision for me and I know she would be right also!

As I sit and hold my Jenny on my lap, I sing to her and I talk to her about our victory we have in Jesus, I quote scriptures that prove Jenny is healed. I love this time Jesus has given me with Jenny. I know I have purpose and purpose gives me a reason to keep going. I know some people think I need a break from care giving but I don't need a break from care giving because my life as a care giver is filled with purpose and purpose gives me joy. Does anyone need a break from Joy? I know I don't!!!

Looking at the calendar I realized Jenny has not had a bowel movement in three days. I checked her bowel cavity and it was empty. I needed to get some cherry juice in Jenny because that always makes her bowel move. When Nurse Diane came today she said I looked even more joyful than usual. I said guess what I have been doing today? She answered with "knowing you that could be anything" I told her I wrote the requirements. She looked puzzled and ask "requirements for what" Jenny's healing of course. Jesus said you have not because you ask not! So I decided to write the requirements now so when Jenny is healed everyone will know Jesus meet every one of the requirements. Nurse Diane looked at the list and smiled; she then said so you want Jenny to be 95 pound bomb shell and have her long hair back so she can put her hair up in a bun and you can tell her she looks wonderful, like you did when she was young!!!!

Then Nurse Diane and I got on to the business at hand. She said she could give Jenny something to make her bowels move. I mentioned that in the past cherry juice has always worked. I have some for Jenny and if I can get her to drink enough her bowels will move good tomorrow.

137

April 26ᵗʰ, 2013

Jenny and I had a really great day. Jenny was able to drink a lot of liquid again today. I spent the entire day feeding Jenny with the eye dropper. I got eight ounces of insure in Jenny and eight ounces of Pedialyte and some more cherry juice. Jenny filled her pamper with urine four times today. I was so happy to see her kidneys working so well. Nurse Diane came by to check on Jenny and I told her how hard it was to check Jenny's bowel, you see for years I have manually unpacked Jenny bowel in the shower. So any mess was easily rinsed down the drain. Nurse Diane said she had another call to go on but on her way back she would stop in and show me how to unpack Jenny while laying Jenny on her side in the bed.

A couple hours later nurse Diane came by and unpacked Jenny while on her side in the bed. It was so easy with two people working together. Jenny just held my hand and I talked to her while Nurse Diane worked. Jenny's stool was soft from the cherry juice and it came out real easy. Again I want to thank God for an easy bowel movement and an easy clean up. I also want to thank God for Nurse Diane and all her help. After Nurse Diane left I Gave Jenny a shower and Jenny stood up better then she has for over a week, another great sign that Jesus is bring Jenny back one day at a time. I really don't care if it takes nine more years or even twenty more years to bring Jenny back, I just love the fact that Jenny is coming back and I thank you Jesus.

Jenny seemed so strong today. I held her on my lap for hours and Jenny responds by relaxing so well. Holding Jenny close and seeing her so comfortable is so rewarding to me. I know if I could only find a way to sleep while holding her on my lap I would hold her all night. I love this time Jesus is giving me and when I say Jesus is my best friend I mean it.

Jesus has provided me with no worries about anything. Jesus gives me peace, so I can hold Jenny for hours and not need or want anything. The peace Jesus gives me is like being in a place I have never been in before. The comfort of this peace is unlike anything I have experienced. I believe Jenny is in this peace and comfort also because she falls asleep so easily. These are big blessings for both of us. I wish I could find a better way to describe my love of Jesus so anyone that reads this book could understand it. If you have read Jenny's Wheelchair book then you know the journey Jenny and I have been on and you know Jesus is my best friend.

April 27th, 2013

I got up early with my Jesus today and wrote a lot of this book. I love my coffee time with my best friend and can't wait to see Jenny healed. I'm so anxious for the healing in Jenny. I hear her little sounds right now so I know she is waking up. Thank you Jesus for more improvement today!

I went back to her bed to hold her and talk to her before I got her up but Jenny's breathing seemed different, it was very faint. I hugged and kissed Jenny like every morning, I gently rubbed her face and caress her face like every morning, I took her covers off one at a time so she could clematises to the temperature of the camper. Then I tried to pick Jenny up and set her on the toilet like I do every morning but this morning it was like nothing I had ever seen before. Picking up Jenny was like trying to pick up a five foot piece of Jell-O without breaking it. This has never happened before. Then I noticed that Jenny's arms were not crossed on her chest and her legs were straight.

I called out to God and asked what is going on Lord? I couldn't believe my eyes; I mean Jenny seemed so much stronger yesterday. I laid her right back in bed, I prayed, I called Don and Lisa the pastor and his wife of the church we attend. I called hospice and they are sending a nurse over. I held Jenny in my arms as I lay beside her in bed but her breathing was so faint. I ask God is the day the day of her healing? I know her healing has to be soon because I never seen Jenny like this before.

Don and Lisa came and we prayed, I continued to stay beside Jenny and hold Jenny; the hospice nurse came. She checked Jenny's pause and said it was fine. She told me, she had seen patients last for months this way. She called the hospice doctor and he prescribed morphine and some drops to put in Jenny's throat, if she started chocking. I apologized to Don and Lisa for getting panicky and I released them to go but thank you Jesus, they wanted to stay. I checked to see if Jenny was soiled and she was not, so I got Jenny up and carried her to the couch and propped her up. I used a den tip to clear Jenny's troth and she stopped gurgling. I tried to get some orange juice down her but she was not awake enough, that is when I realized Jenny's tong was so small I could see beyond her tonsils. I had never been able to see that far down her throat before. I then rearranged her so I could set her on my lap. Jenny went to sleep and she was breathing better. Praise my Jesus!!!

Don and Lisa went to get Jenny's prescriptions. When they came back they stayed again which was great with me. Jenny was awake but still not able to drink. I was only putting a couple drops at a time in the side of her mouth but Jenny would still chock.

Around four in the afternoon I noticed the roof of Jenny's mouth had little white dots on it. I asked Lisa what that meant. She said it is an indication of Jenny's body shutting down. As I put Jenny back on my lap I noticed her foot was discolored; I thought I had bruised Jenny's foot somehow. Thank you Jesus, that Lisa was here; Lisa said it is another indication of the body shutting down. I kept telling myself the miracle must be really close. Jesus must be going to do it right soon. I had been talking about testimonies all day and I kept thinking Jenny's testimony is going to be the greatest testimony I have ever seen.

I told Don and Lisa about Jenny and I having a special song tilled "I will" by Chuck Girard, I explained how the I will song came to be our favorite song and how we should not even sing that song to each other because Jesus sings the "I will" song to us. The refrain is "I will love you forever, and I will need you forever and I will want you forever till thee end of time" in the song Jesus also talks about thoughts He has that are elusive and how these words and thoughts escape him. This really resonates with me because every time Jenny and I go for a walk I sing to Jenny and sometimes the words I sign are so meaningful that I want to write them down, but when I get back to the camper I cannot remember them. Sometimes I would get frustrated at myself because I thought the lyrics where so cool and I wanted to share them. Now I know they were a gift from God and just for Jenny and I at that moment.

After hearing the story about the "I will" song Don said I would like to hear it Ron. I turned it on and because it was already in the CD player, it came on right away. As soon as the music started Jenny's little face transformed in to a big smile, this was a big miracle because Jenny's face mussels had not worked for months. I was so happy to see her smile and then Jenny started crying at the same time. We all were crying so hard, hearing Jesus sing "I will love you forever, I will need you forever and I will want you forever until the end of time" these are the best words I could possibly hear. I just held Jenny and kissed Jenny and told Jenny I love you too. In just thirty or forty seconds Jenny's smile went away and she relaxed in my arms.

When the song was over, we were still crying when I asked Don to turn off the radio. Don and Lisa and I were totally amazed at this amazing blessing from God. It was truly a miracle, a miracle of love. Then I noticed Jenny was not breathing and Lisa got up and checked for Jenny's pause and there was none. I wanted to scream "okay Lord I have waited long enough and now is the time" We called for the hospice nurse, she came and pronounced Jenny's death was 7:20 April 27th 2013. I thought to myself it is time Lord all the witness are here please just RAISE JENNY UP!!! The nurse called someone and gave them the time of death. Then she ask for the drugs and even though the drugs she had ordered just hours ago were never opened and they were still sealed she had to destroy them. She left and that was that.

I continued to hold my Jenny on my lap when Kim came from church. Don had let him know. Kim had prayed for one person to be raised from the dead and that person came back to life. So he started to pray his awesome prayer and I just believed. Then as he was praying I heard loud and clear from my loving Jesus; RON JENNY IS WITH ME NOW!!! I told Kim to stop praying and he did. My delightfully precious Jenny is now the bride of Jesus, but she will always be my delightfully precious Jenny too! I'm sure glade Jesus is in to sharing!

I believe I was in shock. I knew all my life that I never ever had all of Jenny's love because her first love was always Jesus and anyone that needed a big dose of love from Jesus would receive it from Jenny! Jenny never held back her love just like Jesus never

142

holds back His! Jenny was always there for me, always true to me, and will always love me. I told everyone that saw me with my delightfully precious Jenny, how much I am blessed. I don't understand how she could die, I mean I had so many scriptures that say Jenny will be healed. All I really need to know right now, Jesus has already told me "RON JENNY IS WITH ME NOW" what an awesome six words! I do not understand my Jenny is not healed physically or why Jenny is in heaven right now but I am thankful for the knowledge and faith to know Jesus loves me!

I was happy to hear the Hurst was going to take a couple hours to get here. I held Jenny in my arms as we waited; it really felt as though she was just asleep, except her body was cooling down. I just held her closer to keep her warm, I wanted to scream as loud as I could but I knew God was hearing me, I knew God loves me, and I knew that his love will never leave me or forsake me. So I just sat quietly and held my Jenny while I could!!!

I asked Lisa if we should dress Jenny and do her hair. Lisa had told me earlier when her mom died they dressed her real nice and did her hair. Lisa said it was up to me, I selfishly decided to just hold Jenny in my arms. I just could not let Jenny go. Lisa did take Jenny's wedding rings off her finger and set them on the table. The Hearse arrived around 10:30 and at 10:50 I carried Jenny out of the motor home and put her on the stretcher, as they zipped her in the bag and strapped her in I told them not to cover her head and I said if she wakes up on your way to the Science Care place please bring her back!! I put Jenny's book "Jenny's wheelchair, how did we get there" inside the bag so they would know who they were studying.

We went back into the camper and Don asked if I wanted them to stay or go. I said I want to be alone with my Lord for a while and they left, but before they did Don hugged me and said "Ron you did nothing wrong, he said so don't blame yourself. Those were really powerful words and they were really great advice because the devil was already telling me God did not heal Jenny because I didn't deserve a miracle. The devil said I told you, you are nothing. I just kept saying over and over I know you love me Jesus. I know you love me Jesus, I didn't understand how Jenny could die, I mean I had all these promises from my Jesus.

143

By His strips we are healed done deal! These were not just words in a book we call the bible. They are promises from the creator of us all. If you cannot trust His words then what can you trust? I could go on and on about how great my Jesus is and I could quote scriptures that say for sure we are healed. Right now what I need more than anything is time to be alone with my best friend Jesus.

I do know for a fact Jesus loves Jenny and I. I know His words are true and I know Jesus and the Father love Jenny and I and that is really all I need to know. Jesus sees the big picture and I have to trust Him like I say I do, or I will fall into unbelief! I believe Jesus and I will stay in love with Him and I will do His will here on earth. My little Jenny's body was in a Hearse being hauled away. All I could do was cry and try to silence the thoughts I was hearing in my head. Jesus is my best friend, I have proclaimed that to all, I'm a son of God, I'm born again, I live with my brother Jesus' Holy Spirit living in me and Jenny and I have the victory. I know we do, but right now it doesn't seem like it!

Watching Jesus change people's lives is the most joyful, uplifting and fulfilling part of my life! Like I said right now I am hearing all kinds of things in my head, which are not of God and I thank you Jesus that someday I will understand. For now I will keep the faith and think on only those things that are of a good report. Jesus is my best friend and best friends don't leave each other when things don't seem to be right.

I love you Jesus is not just for the good times, it is for the times we don't understand. As the funeral men started zipping Jenny into the body bag I told them not to zip her head in. I told them if she wakes up on the way to the science care lab to call me and I will come and get her or they should bring her back to me.

I sat on the couch where I had held Jenny all day. I was so joyful for my Jenny to be with Jesus and I thanked God for Him telling me. Then I saw her shoes on the floor where I kept them and I busted into tears and said Lord please help me! I just sat there and cried; but as soon as I cried the devil was right there knocking at the door to my heart.! I mean I knew Jenny was in heaven but the thought of not having her with me was unbearable. Jenny and I had been together 24/7 for the last ten years. Then I started to think about Jenny being in heaven, I started to dwell on the fact I knew Jenny was in Heaven and with Jesus. You know the good report Jesus talks about thinking on and I realized the more I dwell on Jenny being in heaven the more thankful I could be! I knew I needed Jesus now more than ever!!! I knew Jesus was with me now more than ever. I could feel my strength coming back. I could feel Joy right here in my camper!!!

The good report is Jenny is in heaven. That is right Jenny is in heaven; the reality is Jenny is in heaven! I called Heidi, Ronnie and Jason, I told them about mom and Ronnie and Jason said dad we will be here in 14 hours. Heidi said she was going to fly into Tallahassee airport and drive down. A little while later I went to bed, but the only way to quite the devil was to keep saying I love you Jesus and I know you love me and Jenny is in heaven. By dwelling on the good report, Jenny was with Jesus I could not be defeated. I went to sleep knowing Jesus loves me so much He told me where Jenny is!

Saturday April 27 2013 will be the end of our forty years, six months, sixteen days and three and a half hours of marriage. This is hard to believe our marriage came to an end and for the first time in over fifteen years I went to bed alone. Jenny and I loved to snuggle up at night but Jenny's body was always to hot for me and I would start to overheat, so every night after our snuggle we would separate but still have to be touching to fall asleep. In 14,799 nights of marriage I bet we weren't apart more than 60 nights. That is an awesome blessing also. I thank you Jesus for loving us so much!!! I thank You Jesus for being my best friend ever!!!

I went to bed by myself and continued to think about all the blessings my wonderful God has given me. Jenny out lived the doctors estimations by four to six years. Even with these extra years I cannot begin to tell you how short life is. Jesus calls life here on earth a vapor of time and He is right. I believe my Jenny is all tucked in and sleeping well in the loving arms of the ultimate, most delightfully precious Jesus, and you know that is where I'm going to sleep someday also. I sure am glade the devil knows his place is a long way form here as long as I believe, because he is doing some pretty loud knocking but I am not lessoning and I

145

know I am worthy of a miracle, not because of anything I did or didn't do. I am worthy of a miracle because Jesus says so in his word. Take that devil, I'm going to sleep.

April 28th, 2013

I'm up and heading to church but truthfully not without a lot of heart ache. I think again how blessed I am but somehow my little delightfully precious Jenny is not here with me and I think, oh dear God please bring her back, I mean you brought Lazars back four days after he died. I will not give up hope! Nothing is impossible for my Jesus! I know if I let my guard down even for a moment I will start to cry but I also know Jenny is in heaven with her first love and that brings me great joy. It is almost like a little war going on in me, if I think about what not having Jenny with me and make life all about me then I am very sad and want to cry. If I think about how great my Jesus is for giving Jenny her final reward then I have Joy beyond belief!

Church was good and Pastor Don prophesied over me, that this is a new beginning; it is a new awareness of seeing with the spiritual eyes of God. I needed to hear his prophesy and it gave me great comfort, I needed to know I will still have purpose. For years I have ask God for His spiritual eyes and for years I believe I have seen people's hearts but now to see as God sees us is not just a request of mine, it is prophesied! Thank You Jesus!!! THANK YOU JESUS!!!

After church Pastor Don and Lisa took me out for lunch, I hope I was not to quite, we sure had some great food and I loved being with them. I know I have Jesus and his love will see me through but it is also wonderful to have real people to love on you also. I thank you Jesus for having Jenny and I here at Carrabelle Beach with so many nice people and for surrounding us with their love.

After lunch with Don and Lisa, I went back to the camper. I was only there a short time and Megan called from Canada. She said her sister who does not know Jenny and I except from Megan

147

telling her about us heard a word from God for us. She was not sure what it meant but the word from Jesus was "Jenny had a choice also." As soon as I heard the word from Jesus everything and I mean everything fell into place. All the promises form God are true, God does heal all, God does raise people from the dead, God does answer prayers, God heard every request I have made for the past ten years and he fulfilled them all. Jenny had the right to use her will just like we all do. Jenny chose Jesus and being with Him in heaven is more comforting to me then having her here with me. I only want the best for my bride, even if giving Jenny the best hurts my heart, my heart rejoices for my Jenny. Heaven is such a fitting place for my Jenny to be, I know Jesus has prepared a special place for her!

As Megan and I talked Megan prophesied over me the same words Don said earlier in church. I almost dropped the phone. They were almost the same exact words. I guess Jesus is trying to tell me something. I still have purpose and Jesus will use me because I am available. Thank you Jesus.

About an hour after talking to Megan I received a phone call from Maylin, she is from North Carolina. I told her about Jenny and we both cried. As we continued talking Maylin prophesied the same words Don said. That is three times in one day. I am sure Jesus has work for me and I am sure I will be ready to do it.

Ronnie and Jason arrived Sunday evening and we talked to about 1;00 am. They went to a motel, the next morning we went to subway for breakfast on St George Island and sat at a picket table where Jenny and I had frequented quite often. It was so nice of them to come and visit me. We shared the love of Jenny and Jesus, which was so beautiful. I will admit I cried when they left but it was really nice to have their love and support. I thank you Jesus for their safe trip down here and back and I thank you boys for coming. 28 hours on the road with a small break in between is a long road trip but my boys made it with smiles on their faces, love in there hearts and that is all I needed. Thank you Jesus.

April 29th, 2013

I decided to write a letter called "Jenny's first love." I wrote it to give to my friends here and to send to friends and relatives. Jenny's last days are so precious and the miracles God performed are so above and beyond anything I could imagine. I can say Jesus loves me, because He proves it to me every day. I am going to insert a copy of the letter "Jenny's first love" here even though you have read some of it in this account.

JENNY'S FIRST LOVE

May 2nd

I find it hard to believe it is already five days since Jenny went to be with Jesus April 27th 2013 at 7:20 pm. I'm in the camper and it seems so empty. I look around and know Jenny will never physically be here again. The camper seems so much bigger. I have given away Jenny's pampers and that freed up space in a cabinet. I looked at my grocery list and could erase about half of it. I know I will have more empty cabinets when I give her clothes away today. We have lived in this thirty-foot camper for four years and two months now and I still had empty drawers while Jenny was alive. I don't know what to do with the space but if I hang onto the memories that come from looking at Jenny's clothes; they bring sadness. So I think I will give Jenny's clothes away; so someone somewhere will have them on and they will bring joyfulness to that person and to all that see them.

I want to talk about Jenny for a moment. About fifteen years ago Jenny started doing some odd behaviors. Eventually Jenny was diagnosed with Picks disease. How did my Jenny get Picks disease and where does it come from, is still a mystery. Picks disease steels your life one ounce at a time. It steels your ability to communicate; it steals your memory, it steals your dignity, in Jenny it stole her walking, her eyesight, her control over bowels and urine and it took the memory of her family!!! Eventually picks disease took her ability to smile, to swallow and to breath. When Jenny left here to go on to her final reward Jenny weighted somewhere between 50 to 60 pounds.

For over nine years I have taken care of Jenny 24/7. A common comment from the beginning of this journey has been "you need to take a break" any book you read about care giving will tell you; "you need to take a break". Two weeks before Jenny died I took her to the emergency room because she had green discharge from her nose. I thank God, Don's wife Lisa recognized Jenny had an infection and told me to take Jenny to the hospital because it was an infection not sinus. The doctor told me, Jenny had the start of pneumonia. He said he could admit Jenny into the hospital for a couple days to give me a break. I told him I don't need a break I just want Jenny's infection cleared up. Pastor Don was there with me and he told the doctor "I have known Ron for four years now and he has never had a break." We were only in the hospital about two hours and Jenny and I were on our way home again. Thank you God for making this a short visit to the hospital. The next day Jenny's infection had cleared up and her breathing was back to normal.

When I called in hospice, the first service they told me about was they could give me a break. I don't know why but I don't need a break. Today I ask my Jesus why I never needed a break, I really didn't know what all this talk about taking breaks was all about. I just knew I didn't need or want one. I decided to go right to my source so I ask my Jesus and Jesus spoke to me and asked me "does anyone need a break from Joy or Love"? Then I understood; Jesus has made care giving to me a Joy and showed me that it is his love. Thank you Jesus and you are right; I don't need a break from YOUR JOY, or YOUR LOVE!!!

Everyone knows I fully expected God to miraculously heal Jenny and the two of us should be together here on earth right now. I thought the joy of Jenny's healing and the miracle of it would be a very strong testimony for the whole world to see and through it we could lead people to Jesus and give Him Glory. I took pictures and had doctor's records and home movies, in other words I had proof of how sick Jenny was, so with all this evidence Jenny's healing was going to be an undeniable miracle. I just stood in faith and didn't look at my circumstances. I know the word of God says He heals all! Even the hospice nurses new my faith was for Jenny's miracle. I professed it to all and never wavered. SO HOW COULD JENNY DIE? Then when Jenny did die I though okay Jesus is going to raise her from the dead, WOW! EVEN A BIGGER MIRACLE!!! As you know that didn't happen.

151

After the body was hauled away, Pastor Don hugged me and said you did nothing wrong Ron, don't blame yourself. Those were the best and most powerful words anyone could of said to me because I was already hearing from the devil. The devil was already shouting in my ear, you are not deserving, you never where, I told you your nothing. My child hood was flashing in front me and memories of sins were bombarding me. I started praying and praying and praying and praying some more!

I ask God to talk to me! Then I realized God had talked to me already. Yes God had used the voice of Don to talk over the devil and tell me I have done nothing wrong. Suddenly I could see how big My Jesus is and how big His forgiveness is! Isn't GOD GOOD! THANK YOU GOD FOR YOUR LOVE FOR JENNY AND I!!! THANK YOU JESUS FOR LOVING ME!!!!

After they left I kept saying I know you love me Jesus. I really don't understand any of this; but I know you love me Jesus. I bet I said it a thousand times, I know you love me and your love is all I need. I said it loud to get over the other voice in my head. I kept saying it until I fell asleep. I know you love me Jesus!!! I know it was the love of Jesus that got me through that night!! Thank you Jesus for loving me so much.

Today I was packaging up some of the "Jenny's Wheelchair" books to send to friends; when Jesus prompted me to send one of our friends a teaching Jesus and I wrote a while ago. I didn't know which teaching he needed so I went to the car; looked into my file and said, "Okay Lord which one?" Jesus said, "FRUITS." Before I put the Fruits teaching in the envelope; Jesus said, "Read it." So I did! It is all about recognizing the Fruits from God and discerning our thoughts. As I read it God was reminding me of the Hero's teaching also. Both talk about motive and how motive affects the outcome of your prayers and actions.

I was reading the Fruits teaching when Jesus spoke to me again! Jesus asked, "What was your motive for marrying Jenny?" I said, "To bring her joy, to provide for her and together for us to build a love so strong it would hold us together no matter what life brings. We wanted a love that will last the rest of our lives, and as you know Jesus heard our prayers and answered them.

When I met Jenny, she was in a foster home and I wanted to give her security and a place to live. I wanted to watch us grow together, love together, be together, to have children and watch them grow. I wanted to protect Jenny from all harm and be with her always!

Then Jesus asked me, "What was your motive for the last ten years while you took care of your Jenny." I said, "To bring her to a place of your healing and to make her as comfortable and joyful as possible until her healing manifest, here on earth." I said, "You know Jesus I wanted her to see how you changed me from flesh that should need a break, to spiritual that never grows weary. I wanted Jenny to see how your love for us transformed us into the image and likeness of YOU! I wanted her to see the new me, you made me into. I wanted Jenny to have coffee with you and me, Jesus! I wanted Jenny to be free of Picks disease. To smile, to love, to laugh, to run, to have and know her family again, and most of all for us together to share you Jesus and Your love to the world!"

Then Jesus said, "Did you succeed in your goals?"

Just then I realized all the goals and more are met and Jenny is more joyful then I could have made her here on earth, Jesus showed me Jenny is safe in His arms now and no harm can come to her ever. If Jenny was healed 100% here on earth she could not be as joyful as she is right now. Nothing we could ever do here on earth could even come close to the joy of being face to face with my Jesus. Jesus showed me all my goals are achieved! We, that is Jesus, Jenny and I have the VICTORY! Yes Jesus made all the goals and more come true. THANK YOU JESUS FOR SHOWING ME ALL YOUR PROMISES ARE TRUE!! I LOVE YOU TOO!!!

The night Jenny went to be with Jesus, Kim Allen came over and was praying for Jenny to come back from the dead. As He prayed I heard Jesus say, "Ron, Jenny is with me now" I told Kim to stop praying. The next day I heard from Megan (a friend in Canada) that God told her sister during the night to tell Ron "Jenny had the right to choose also". As soon as I heard those words I remembered Pastor Don telling me about his mother and how he released her to be with Jesus. His mother cried and said,

153

"You know Don I will always love you, but I love Jesus more than anyone on earth." I know Jenny loves me and I know Jenny's first love was and always will be Jesus. Jenny very intelligently and with full mental capacity chose Jesus and I know she made the right choice!

At some point that night I started telling Don and Lisa about the "I will" song by Chuck Girard. This song was our favorite song. The refrain is "I will love you forever, I will need you forever and I will want you forever until the end of time!" I know now it was the Holy Spirit talking through Don when he ask me to play the song. The CD was already in the radio so I turned it on and when the music started Jenny's face lit up. Jenny suddenly smiled at me and started crying, she was able to hold her smile for at least thirty seconds and we all started crying, I told Jenny I love you over and over. When the song was over I had Jenny on my lap, in my arms, and holding her as close as I could! Then I noticed Jenny was not breathing and Lisa checked and there was no pause. Jenny went home to be with Jesus, her first love! Pastor Don and Lisa where there with me and I thank God for them being there! They witness Jenny's last act of kindness and Jesus blessed me with knowing even picks disease could not steel Jenny's love for me!!! I know Jenny is with Jesus and that is as sweet as life can get!!!

Everything I prayed for came true and all though my hopes were for a physical healing and for us to be together I know Jenny's choice should be and was Jesus and I know Jesus has always been; Jenny's first love!

A lot of people have said Jenny was healed in heaven and I want you to know I don't agree with that. I mean I don't think there are any hospitals in heaven. Jenny's spirit was never sick and so Jenny's spirit never needed healing.

I thank you Jesus for the "I Will" song and the miracle of Jenny's smile; that came fourth so big and bright, to let me know how much Jenny loved me! I thank you Jesus for the tears form Jenny's eyes that showed me how much her heart wanted to stay! I want to thank you Jesus for letting me hold Jenny on my lap and letting her know how much she was loved right up to the last second. Jesus you are so beautiful to me!!!

I thank you Jesus for telling me that Jenny was with you and putting to rest any doubt. I thank you Jesus for telling me that Jenny chose You and for showing me how all my dreams for her have come true. I thank You Jesus for teaching me; the most important relationship anyone can have is with You. I thank You Jesus that Jenny did not need any narcotics, or drugs of any kind. Jesus; you are Jenny's first love and You will be forever; my first love too!!!

Jesus gave Jenny the most beautiful transition anyone could ask for! Jesus showed me all His promises are true and being true to his word Jesus allowed Jenny her desire to be with Him. Today I am so secure knowing Jenny is in His arms and He is telling Jenny how much she is loved and I can rest knowing I have this awesome relationship with My Jesus too! I know the word father means to come forth from and the word God means the source of life. I know Jenny is with her Father whom we all came forth from and is the source of life! That is the peace Jesus promised that surpasses all understanding and it is the Joy that will propel me to continue on; until Jesus calls me home.

Being with Jesus is heaven and heaven is knowing Jenny is in the loving arms of My Jesus!!! "JENNY'S FIRST LOVE" thank you Jesus, I love you too!!!

My delightfully precious Jenny went to be with our precious Lord April 27 2013 at 7: 20pm! Jenny's leaving was her choice not the work of picks disease! Praise you Jesus for such a special and fitting transition! Jenny never showed any pain, had no shortness of breath and was in my arms until the last second!!! These are really big gifts from my delightfully precious Jesus!!!!

A couple years ago while having coffee with my best friend Jesus; I ask Him "Jesus I always call my Jenny precious but I would like to know how you refer to Jenny?" Immediately I heard the words "delightfully precious" I thought I agree, Jenny is totally delightfully precious to me too!!!!

Thank You Jesus for this awesome Journey, for wisdom to know how to tend to Jenny, for understanding and grace you flowed through Jenny to me and for the faith to be in your presents continually!!! Thank you for the hope that I too will come home to see you and be with you someday. I guess you get the picture, I am thankful for my forty years, six months, sixteen days, and three hours of marriage to my most delightfully precious Jenny! It just was not enough, but then I guess it was!! My delightfully precious Jenny is with My delightfully precious Jesus!! I will remain forever thankful to you Jesus and to all that helped us along the way!!!

To sum things up Jesus talked to me six times, in less then 24 hours.

- First, was with the "I will song to show how much Jenny loved me and wanted to express that love!"

- Second, when Jesus said "Jenny is with me now"! So I knew not to keep trying to raise Jenny from the dead.

- Third, when he had Pastor Don say "you did nothing wrong." The devil is knocking every day with what I could perceive as something I didn't do right but I put Jesus in my mind and don't give those thoughts time to raise any doubt.

- Fourth, when Megan called to say "Jenny had a choice also"! That is right, Jenny had a choice and she rightfully chose Jesus!

- Fifth, was when three different people prophesied, on Sunday. Pastor Don prophesied in church; then Maylin form North Carolina called me right after church and said almost the exact words Don used and then Megan called form Canada with the exact prophesy Don had!

- Sixth was going on all my life and continues still today! Jesus told me how much He loves us and He is still telling me How Much He Loves Me today. Because of His love I have Purpose and peace knowing I did nothing wrong! Jesus gave the desire to take care of Jenny right to the end and then Jesus fulfilled that desire and allowed Jenny to be in my arms smiling and crying right up to the last second of her life!!! I am the most blessed man on earth; I have relationship with my Jesus and life cannot get any better than that!!!! Jesus is my best friend and He proves it every day!!!

To me love is the most powerful force on earth. I can say that without any reservations because Jesus said He came to show us the Father and all Jesus did was show us love every second of His life. Jesus forgave all and loved all through that forgiveness. So I know without a doubt that His love will see me through and carry me on to new days filled with His kingdom work! Jesus is our example and I will follow Him no matter what the cross looks like.

April 30ᵗʰ, 2013

Four days have passed and I realized Jesus waited four day until He raised Lazarus up! I thought Jesus razed Lazarus from the dead in four days so why not Jenny. The fourth day came and went without a phone call from my delightfully precious Jenny and no sighting either. I know all things are possible and just because Jenny's body is in the science lab doesn't mean Jesus won't raise her up. I love you Jesus and I know it was Jenny's will to be with you and I know Jenny made the right choice. I'm just holding on to a little hope that she might change her mind and you would grant her wish. I will say having the knowledge of Jenny being in heaven is the most comforting, peaceful wonderful thoughts I can have.

I thank you also for the knowledge and wisdom to know some big changes are coming for us here in America and it is a real comfort to know no one and I mean nothing and no one, can hurt my Jenny. I Thank You Jesus for the revelations and the wisdom but most of all to know your love will see me through the years ahead.

Don and Lisa had me over for dinner tonight. I sure enjoy being with them. They have a special way of making you feel loved and they are both so knowledgeable. I feel really privileged and honored to get to spend time with them. I hope someday to be as great an example of the love of Jesus as they are.

To sum things up, I am still the most blessed man in the world. I have the love of Jesus in my heart and I know Jenny is with our FIRST LOVE. Life really cannot get any better than that!!! I know that loving Jesus and knowing Jesus is the joy that surpasses all understanding. I know the Joy of knowing Jesus is more than a bus ticket to heaven. I know Jesus said we can bring Heaven to earth and having a relationship with Jesus is being in

158

Heaven right now. Thank You Jesus for your love and for allowing me to be in heaven right now!

May 18th, 2013

Today while having coffee with my Jesus I noticed Jenny's Wheelchair book setting on the couch. I felt prompted so I picked up Jenny's book and opened it to page 48, just a random pick. I started reading, the first paragraph says

"I remember in October of 07 Jenny and I were in the living room and Jenny said I want home. I said Jenny we are home. Jenny got frustrated and said I want home. I said Jenny we are home. Then Jenny said I want Jesus home go to. I said you want to go to heaven and see Jesus and Jenny smiled. I said you will but I want you here for a long time. Jenny looked like she understood and just put her head down and said ok."

Today I cried as I read about my Jenny wanting to go home and I realized that was almost six years ago, Jenny ask to go home. Jesus never ceases to bless me and amaze me. I mean Jesus gave me almost six extra years with My Jenny, and now realizing and knowing Jenny had ask to go home in October of 07. Thank you Jesus for all the time you gave me with my delightfully precious Jenny. Thank you my delightfully precious Jesus for making us in your image and likeness. Thank you for forty years six months sixteen days and three hours of marriage to your delightfully precious Jenny. JESUS I WILL LOVE YOU FOREVER UNTIL THE END OF TIME!!!!!

May 20th, 2013

It has already been three weeks since Jenny went to be with Jesus and looking back I have realized what a blessing I received from my Jesus, that is when Jesus said these six words "Ron, Jenny is with me now". How many people never know for sure where there loved one is and yet Jesus blessed me with this wisdom. Those are the most powerful, the most wonderful; the most blessed words anyone could hear form their creator and best friend Jesus. Jesus I love you with all my heart and Jesus I love you forever.

Also as I think back over the years I remember when Jenny and I first started dating and how I literally could not be with Jenny enough. I looked so forward to being with her. I don't remember ever asking God is Jenny the right girl for me? I do remember asking God can I make Jenny happy the rest of her life? Can we be a joy to each other forever? I had doubts about providing a good home for Jenny but I never doubted our love!

I remember our honeymoon like it was yesterday. I remember when I went back to work after our honeymoon was over. I worked at Procter and Gamble, the night shift from four in the afternoon until midnight. At midnight, I was always the first one out the door and the first car out of the parking lot every night. After a couple weeks of this some of my co-workers ask me during our lunch break if I thought my wife Jenny was cheating on me.

I was totally surprised by their question! They explained how I ran to the car every night and speed out of the parking lot, made them wonder if I thought Jenny might be having an affair on me. They thought I was trying to catch her in the act. I said guys; I just cannot wait to see my Jenny, she waits up every night to see me too! Those nights were really wonderful, the time we shared our hopes and dreams for the future. Jenny would always have

161

something for me to eat and because it was midnight we didn't have a lot of distractions, like phone calls etc, so we really enjoyed that time together. The men looked surprised by my answer and I think there might have been a little envy also.

I don't think anyone realizes what we have until it is gone. My physical time with Jenny is over and that is so hard to believe, waking up without Jenny next to me is as lonely as live can get. Going to bed without Jenny is the hardest thing I think I have ever done. To live without her is like trying to live without my heart. The void in my heart can only be filled with love, nothing but love, nothing satisfies like the true love of Jesus, that is why I will continue to seek God with all my heart and He is rewarding me with His love!!! I believe I could of laid down my life for Jenny just as Jesus did for us. I believe Jesus made my Jenny's love so special to me and through her love I have tasted a small taste, yes I would say a vapor of the love Jesus has for us. I believe I am loved by Jesus and Father God and although their love is not physical, it satisfies my spirit and our spirit is truly the only place we can experience love.

THANK YOU JESUS FOR YOUR LOVE!!!!

May 28th, 2013

It is really weird to think about Jenny being gone thirty days already. I know Jenny is in heaven and as you know that brings great peace to me. Now I have a different set of problems to contend with. While Jenny was alive no one ever ask how do you do a wheel chair in the camper, or where is your wheel chair lift? No one ever ask those questions because they saw me carry Jenny in and out of the camper all the time. Now without Jenny here those questions are coming up. I thought, most people that read this book would like to know also. My camper is a 1995 motor home without slide outs. The walkways inside are very narrow. This was never a problem for Jenny and I, because I could just carry her to the bathroom or to bed etc. I hope that explains how I got Jenny around in the camper.

I did modify the camper a little. The bathroom door was to small. I originally took it off the hinges and that gave me about another inch and a half of opening. This proved not to be enough so I took out a wall between the bath and bedroom. It was not that big of a deal except for the wiring in that wall. The section I took out had two light switches in it, one for the bedroom light and one for the bathroom light. There was a 12 volt plug for a television and an antenna connection for the television. Also in the wall was a 110 volt receptacle and a floor marker light, that is a special light near the floor that you could turn on at night while driving, so some someone could walk around and see where they were going, without the light bothering the driver. Also there was lot of wiring going into the ceiling for lights and the air conditioning unit in the bedroom. If that was not enough there was also an accordion door that would shut for privacy from the bedroom while showering. We did not need that either so it went with the wall.

Jesus and I wrote another paper about my thoughts thirty two days after Jenny passed.

RON'S FIRST LOVE

May 29th 2013

Wow it has been 32 days already, Jenny is in heaven with my Jesus and I am so Joyful for her! I have been trying to figure out what the proper response is to Jenny's death. I mean people that knew Jenny and my relationship will never question my love for Jenny. Now with Jenny at home with you Jesus, people I meet do not get to witness our love flowing through and between us. I don't know if this is imagined or not but some people seem to question my love for Jenny when they see me Joyful so soon after her death.

Right after Jenny passed I tried to stay busy and found that was not the answer. I slept more those first couple weeks, then I ever have slept. Sleep was not the answer. I went across the street to the park where Jenny and I have walked and prayed for people to be healed for four years now. I wanted to see if I could find someone to pray for, there was one person in the park so I approached her and we did have some good conversation about Jesus. She even came to church that Sunday. I just new in my heart I was not quite ready to pray for others just yet. So I went to my source and ask God "where am I missing it?" Jesus said "seek you first the Kingdom of God!" I thought you're right as usual Lord I haven't been seeking you the way I should be. I started seeking God, not for sympathy or answers but for our relationship again.

I thank God I have a relationship with Him. When I started really seeking God full time again I really started receiving healing to my heart and I am Joyfully announcing to all; I have the Joy of the Lord back!! It might be 30 years before I see Jesus and Father face to face but it will happen and it will be even a bigger party because I know they will wait until there timing of my going home is there perfect timing, like they did my Jenny. That is correct; I believe Jenny's going home to be with Jesus was the right perfect timing of my Jesus!!! Thank You Jesus for your perfect love and for letting me see your perfect love that protects Jenny forever!

When you seek Jesus first in your life you will have the Spirit of Joy dwelling in you. Jesus said the Joy of the Lord will be our strength. I have Joy because Jesus gave me conformation as to where Jenny is spending eternity, not that there was any doubt, but because Jesus loves me so much He removed all the temptations from the devil to have me think differently! I am joyful because I know Jenny is in the loving, safety of my Father and Jesus. I am Joyful because I know absolutely no harm can ever hurt my Jenny again. I am Joyful and I give thanks to my Jesus for taking Jenny home to be with Him. That's right I am giving thanks to my Jesus for taking Jenny home, I realize nothing and no one can even come close to the Love Jenny is experiencing right now. With the knowledge of knowing Jenny is home with Jesus "Her first love", how can I not be joyful?

Even if I live here on earth another 30 years it is just a blink of an eye to eternity. I obviously have more work to do here on earth and with the Holy Spirit dwelling in me, I am up for the challenge, whatever that challenge is! I have the Holy Spirit living in me, dwelling in me, and I hear the voice of my God guiding me every day. If that doesn't bring Joy in your life you must be clueless.

I have purpose and Kingdom work to do, I have the power to heal the sick flowing through me, I have the power to raise the dead working in me, and the power to cast out devils and power to set people free. These are real powers and in the name of Jesus I will watch the Holy Spirit perform these miracles.

Jesus is more real now after Jenny's passing then before her passing. Dan Mohler once said in one of his talks, trials to our faith will come our way, but the trial the devil is using to try to break you with; (destroying your faith) he (the devil) runs the risk of that trial making you (building your faith).

For example; after praying and believing and standing in faith, that Jesus would physically heal Jenny, I believe the devil thought he could use Jenny's death to break my faith in Jesus. I'm not saying the devil killed Jenny, I don't believe the devil has that power, unless we give him the power. I'm saying the devil is am opportunist and being an opportunist he saw an open door when Jenny went to heaven and he jumped at the chance to tell me Jesus did not heal Jenny because of some unworthiness on my part.

It has been 32 days since Jenny went to be with Jesus and the devil is still trying to tell me it was my fault Jenny was not healed. When I was young I used to lesson to the devil when he told me I was a slow learner, and so I thought I was a slow learner. I used to lesson when the devil would tell me I was to stupid to get good grades in school. Do you get the picture I'm trying to paint? The devil will tear you down and make you feel worthless, if you let him. The devil will destroy you if you lesson to him.

I was reading this letter to Pastor Don and he gave me this verse, I think it is so appropriate to show or explain the meaning I am trying to convey. Thank you Don and thank you Jesus for the friends like Don in my life.

1Pe 5:8 Be sober, be vigilant; because your adversary the devil, as a roaring lion, walketh about, seeking whom he may devour:

Pastor Don was very quick to point out that the devil is not a roaring lion, the scripture says as AS, as in as, so do not give the devil any power, the devil has no power over your life except the power you give Him, when you start lessoning to him. The scripture says the devil walketh about seeking whom he may devour. See the words may devour, the devil cannot devour you unless you lesson to him and give him the power or permission to devour you. That is why I will focus on Jesus and keep my mind on Jesus and the perfect love of Jesus that cast out all fear. Like I said the devil was talking to me and the devil will talk to you, that is why we must learn to DISCERN our thoughts.

I mentioned Jesus talked through Pastor Don to me a couple times. Even though I trust Don to be a great friend and know his heart is to hear from God and to flow God's word on to me, I still have to use discernment. I believe discernment is one of the biggest and best gifts the Holy Spirit can give you. Lord I thank You for the gift of discernment.

The perfect love of Jesus is knowing the truth that I am a child of God, I am loved by God, yes Jesus loves me, Jesus never created a slow learner or anyone useless! I am born again, so I am born into the image and likeness of God. I am no longer restrained by the original sin of Adam, I am free to be who God created me to be and I am free to love Jesus with all my heart. We all have purpose and if we really get the understanding that Jesus died to show us how much He loves us and Jesus died to restore our relationship to Him, we will all be in a better place and the world will not be able to hurt us ever.

Just as when I was younger and heard the voice of the devil talking to me, destroying me ever so slowly, I now hear the words of Jesus saying I created you in my image and likeness. The image of God is love and the likeness of God is to share the love of Jesus to all you meet. I get up in the morning and I'm excited, I'm ready to share the love of Jesus, I am ready to be the love of Jesus to all. That makes me Joyful no matter what my circumstances are.

When Father God Took Lazarus Home.

Can you imagine Jesus saying and praying and asking His Father (why did you let Lazarus die? Why did this happen? Why was I not there? Why why why?) Come on now those why words would sound stupid coming out of the mouth of Jesus and they should sound just as stupid coming out of the mouths of believers. Jesus the man was just a believer like us, tempted just like us, and at times heartbroken just like us.

Yes the devil will be right there from time to time to try to talk you out of sharing God's love, but you and I do not have to lesson to him. We simply have a choice to make! I do not have to fight the devil I just simply trust in the love of God, you too can trust in God who sent His Son to show us His love. Any time you hear a voice in your head that belittles you, tears you down or says you are not worthy, check your source, Jesus said He will never leave you or forsake you, and I believe Jesus.

Believe in Jesus and trust in Jesus and watch the devil run to find greener pastures, who are the greener pastures for the devil, anyone that doesn't know the love of Jesus: that is someone that has not meet YOU yet. YOU are alive to Show the love of Jesus and to BE the Love of Jesus to the world and with the love of Jesus YOU can make the devil find a completely different world to do his dirty work in. When you show people love and when you are the walking, talking love of Jesus I know people will notice and they will want what you have.

We are to be the representative of the love of Jesus; Jesus will flow through you to others. When people see the love of Jesus in you they will want what you have and you can freely give your love and not worry about rejection because yourself worth comes form

God who will never reject you. Can you even imagine Jesus worried about rejection; Jesus knew the love of our Father so He never worried about rejection and neither should you. I know I am loved, do you?? Jesus NEVER made life about himself.

Yes Jenny died and for a week or two I was very sad, yes I have been sad to the point of crying, I realized every time I cried, I was making life about me and life is not about me. When life becomes all about me the devil can get his foot in the door to my heart and it is very hard to shut a door when someones foot is in it. Never make life about you or yourself because selfishness has nothing to do with God. Selfishness is sinfulness to the max, selfishness is totally ungodly because God is love and in the bible love is actually translated as Charity. Jesus said "but the greatest of these is charity"

1Co 13:13 And now abideth faith, hope, charity, these three; but the greatest of these is charity.

Charity has nothing to do with selfishness. Thanks to Jesus there is so much of God's grace to see us through and the love of God is stronger than any grief.

When I decided to give Jenny's clothes away, I folded each piece and I cried as I remembered her wearing each outfit. There was real pain in my heart and there was a voice in me that said hold on to the clothes, it's all you have left. I placed them in the bags and carried them to the car and I cried the whole time. I actually wanted to hold onto the pain for some reason, (who was I lessoning to?) I wanted to feel the loss so bad, I wanted the hurt to explode my heart. I wanted to be with my Jenny!!!! Do you hear all the I's in that paragraph? This paragraph is all about me and that is sadness to the max.

I drove to the church that would find needy people and give them Jenny's clothes. As I pulled away from the church I felt as though a big burden was lifted. I realized all the pain from looking at Jenny's clothes was gone and wanting my heart to explode was gone also. I realized I was no longer making this all about me and I realized I had no need for sympathy. I realized when life is all about yourself, pain can be your friend because people will feed that pain by saying "oh look he is so hurting, or his pain is the worst I ever seen!" I can tell you sympathy is nothing but a big zero and zero times anything is still zero! That is why anyone who needs sympathy will always need more sympathy!

Please don't get me wrong, Jesus showed compassion toward others and Jesus sent us a comforter (the Holy Spirit). The difference between the good compassion of Jesus and the devils counterfeit sympathy is the compassion form God lifts you up and makes you sore on the wings of angles. The compassion from God moves you past the hurt and pain of the problem or loss of the loved one. Where the counterfeit (the devils sympathy) just brings more sadness and attention to your own selfish needs. I will not go there; instead I will dwell on the fact that Jenny is in the loving arms of my Jesus! I do not need sympathy when I think of Jenny being with Jesus! I will dwell on being like Jesus and doing whatever he has for me to do today. I do not need sympathy because I have purpose! Thank You Jesus!!!!

Jesus gave me an example of compassion verses sympathy! If your mom went into the hospital and the doctor said, to save her life we must cut off your legs. A minute later, In walks someone from a church and says can I pray for you, he prays; Lord let the doctor do a good job, let the recovery be swift and help her find the resources to buy a great wheelchair. You thank jim fro the beautiful prayer. An hour latter another guy form a different church walks in and ask to pray for your mom. He prays Lord in the name of Jesus I command this spirit of infirmity to go! I command this woman to get up and walk! Then he grabs her hand and says get up and walk now! I bet everyone would say the sympathy of the first prayer would be received just like the doctors report. The second prayer, the prayer of compassion would be rejected and people would ask who does he think he is. They would probably say if he comes back don't let him in he just upset mom.

I ask who is more Christ like the first or the second person to pray. I tell you the devil has turned the action of compassion into sympathy and if your mother has her legs cut off and she lives, you will give the credit to the doctors. I don't see anywhere in the bible where Jesus ever prayed for the doctors to do a good job.

Read these verses from Peter and see real Hope Faith and Charity can be and how Hope, Faith and Charity replace the need for sympathy

1Pe 1:3 Blessed be the God and Father of our Lord Jesus Christ, which according to his abundant mercy hath begotten us again unto a lively hope by the resurrection of Jesus Christ from the dead,

We should bless God all the time because of His abundant mercy. It is His mercy on us His creation that gives us a lively hope for eternal life through the resurrection of my loving Jesus Christ. I have a lively Hope and trust that Jesus will dwell in me forever. I have a lively Hope that the same Spirit that raised Jesus from the dead (defeated death) lives inside me. With blessings of a lively hope who needs money or earthly junk. I am the most blessed man I know. Jesus is alive and well, dwelling in side me and I love our relationship.

1Pe 1:4 To an inheritance incorruptible, and undefiled, and that fadeth not away, reserved in heaven for you,

You see how that makes giving Jenny's clothes away the right thing to do. We have an inheritance that is incorruptible and undefiled, my inheritance is knowing Jenny is in the loving arms of Jesus. Knowing Jenny is in heaven is incorruptible and undefilable and that is true Joy now! That is heaven now! Our inheritance is reserved in heaven if we give up the earthly desires now. So why should I hold on to the sympathy that comes from looking at her clothes and the sad memories they bring.

If you read JENNY'S WHEELCHAIR book you will know I have a treasure chest of great promises God gave me to hold on to and they bring great Joy, they bring great hope and they bring the love of my Jesus home to me now! I have the inheritance of the love of my Father and the love of my Jesus and most of all I have it right now through the Holy Spirit that dwells in me now! Jesus said to bring heaven to earth and I have heaven right now! If I hold on to earthy junk I will miss my heaven now! I will miss my comfort now! I will miss God's plan for my life and that would be a big tragedy! I will never trade God's love for the momentary satisfaction of someones sympathy or earthy junk!

1Pe 1:5 Who are kept by the power of God through faith unto salvation ready to be revealed in the last time.

We are the kept and by the power of belief in God through faith we will receive our salvation and Jesus can reveal it to our loved ones here on earth. Thank You Jesus for revealing Jenny is in heaven!! There is nothing on earth that can come close to the freedom and peace that comes from a heart to heart relationship with God. I will not let anything come between my heart and the heart of my Jesus, I have His Holy Spirit in me and I love it!

1Pe 1:6 Wherein ye greatly rejoice, though now for a season, if need be, ye are in heaviness through manifold temptations:

Yes I do rejoice, yes I am rejoicing and yes I am in a season of heaviness from the loss of My Jenny but I will resist the temptations to be depressed (in need of sympathy) for I am useless to everyone when I only think of myself. I can guarantee you anyone that is depressed is only thinking of what they want in life and even if they got 99% of everything they wanted they would still be depressed. I refuse to let the loss on my Jenny dictate my feelings! I refuse to let my circumstances dictate my Joy or lack of it. I will rejoice knowing I have a loving brother who is my best friend!!! I am rejoicing in the love of my Jesus and I rejoice in our personal heart to heart relationship.

1Pe 1:7 That the trial of your faith, being much more precious than of gold that perisheth, though it be tried with fire, might be found unto praise and honour and glory at the appearing of Jesus Christ:

Life is a trial of Faith, but thank you Jesus I am more precious than gold and I will be found to be praise worthy and like gold, I will not smell like the fire that purifies me; I will give honor and glory to God who gave me the faith to use in times like these. Faith is like love, it is to flow through us not just to us. So you go God, I am a believer and signs and wonders will follow me wherever the Two of us go! Praise you my Jesus and my Father God for all your sacrifices and for giving your Holy Spirit to anyone that asks for Him!!!! That is right the Holy Spirit is there for anyone that seeks a relationship with Jesus. Notice I did not say He is there because you went to church, the Holy Spirit is there for anyone that spends time seeking Him. Talk to God about what God needs done today and He will tell you, I have the Joy of my Jesus not the momentary happiness of the world.

Jesus, Your word says you are no respecter of persons and believing in your word, I believe you will give your Holy Spirit to anyone that asks for it. What a gift to give away, your word says freely you receive and free you give. I know everyone can have Him, if they just believe, the problem is most people want to use your gift to just have a better day for themselves. Their faith is for a blessing daily, I hear people pray for momentary things, like money, a better car, a bigger house and their children are watching television all day while both their parents are out working two jobs. Our prayer should be what we can do for you Jesus, Yes our prayer should be to do the work of the kingdom, and forget the junk of this world and lets spend time with our children. I mean if you do not show your children who Jesus is; then who will? I know television will not!!!! I know Jesus trusted you with temporary guardianship of His children and it is up to you to show them Jesus in word and deed!

Dearest Jesus I pray for more selflessness in my life. I pray that I never get in your way. That is I pray that whatever you want done today I will give you the time you need to do it. I pray to be an example of your love; actually, I pray to be your love! Thank You Jesus for being love and showing that love is the supernatural force that moves mountains. Thank you Jesus that we can and will move some mountains today and together we will cast them in to the sea like your word says. Thank you Jesus I have compassion and not sympathy to give to others. Thank You Jesus for Your good example for all to see! Thank You Jesus, You love me!!! Thank You Jesus that your love is purifying me and renewing my mind daily, so I can walk boldly knowing You are who I want to be!

I know you know by now but I'm going to say it any way, Thank You Jesus for being my best friend and forever you will be MY FIRST LOVE.

Everyone that knows me knows I have my coffee with Jesus every morning and they know I communion with Jesus all day through. The other morning a friend, Maylin was telling her little boy, who ask her what she was doing, at five o clock in the morning? I'm having coffee with Jesus and then she ask her little boy if he wanted to join her in conversation with Jesus? The little boy excitedly said yes but I think Jesus would like some scrambled eggs. I honestly love the honesty of little children.

Jenny, Ron and Jesus will love you forever until the end of time, so be blessed and seek the Lord with all your heart.

I pray for you to have your best day ever by having some heart to heart time with Your best friend and mine, Jesus.

P.S. I think Maylin's little boy is right! Jesus would like some scrambled eggs with His coffee!

THE CLOSING

I believe it is time to close this book on Jenny's life. I know Jenny's little life has made an impact on others because Jenny is a 100% giver of love, just like Jesus. I hope and pray that after reading this book you are inspired to know Jesus on deeper level and have a real relationship with Him! Truly life has no meaning without Jesus. Closing this book is really hard for me; it is like ending Jenny's life again!

The good news is Jesus has inspirited me to right another book about Jenny. This one will start with the beginning of Jenny's life. Over the years I have collected information about the younger years of Jenny's life in the foster homes. This was not easy because Jenny never talked much about those years. I think what I do have will be worth sharing and hopefully help others to be overcomers like Jenny was. I do know Jenny was more than a wife to me; Jenny was an inspiration and I thank God for these wonderful years together. Yes thank You Jesus for this time with your delightful precious Jenny!!!! I love you Jenny and look forward to coffee time in heaven with you and Jesus and Father God!!!! Thank You Jesus for making Jenny your bride!!!! Thank You Jesus for these precious years with YOUR JENNY!!!!

Jesus and I love you forever, until the end of time!

Like I tell everyone, for a little bit of heaven call

(513)377-1727

www.CoffeeTimeWithJesus.com

10032263R00100

Made in the USA
San Bernardino, CA
03 April 2014